New York

A Pictorial Celebration

by Rebeccah Welch, Ph.D.

Photography by Elan Penn

Sterling Publishing Co., Inc.
New York

Design by Michel Opatowski
Edited by Rachel Penn
Copyedited Jacqueline Mulhern
Layout by Gala Pre Press Ltd.

Certain introduction passages and site histories by editor

Penn Publishing gratefully acknowledges the following institutions and individuals
for allowing photographs from their collections to be reproduced in this book:

Alan Schein Photography/Corbis 73, 90, 145, 151, 155
Barbara Alper courtesy of Brooklyn Botanic Garden 55
Bo Zaunders/Corbis 113
Brooklyn Museum:
Adam Husted 101
James Gordon 101
D. DeMello © Wildlife Conservation Society 52
Duomo/Corbis 88
Eleanor Bentall/Corbis 79
Ellen Labenski @ The Solomon R. Guggenheim Foundation 116
J. Maher © Wildlife Conservation Society 53
Joseph Sohm; Visions of America/Corbis 44
Library of Congress 6, 7, 8, 9, 12, 13, 14, 15, 16, 17, 18, 19, 23
Metropolitan Museum of Art 100
Brooks Walker 108
Michael S. Yamashita/Corbis 96
New York Public Library 10, 11, 21, 22
Richard H. Cohen /Corbis 150
Rudy Sulgan/Corbis 122
The Frick Collection 103
The Metropolitan Opera 107

Library of Congress Cataloging-in-Publication Data Available

2   4   6   8   10   9   7   5   3   1

Published by Sterling Publishing Co., Inc.
387 Park Avenue South, New York, NY 10016
Copyright © 2007 Penn Publishing Ltd.
Distributed in Canada by Sterling Publishing
c/o Canadian Manda Group, 165 Dufferin Street,
Toronto, Ontario, Canada M6K 3H6
Distributed in the United Kingdom by GMC Distribution Services,
Castle Place, 166 High Street, Lewes, East Sussex, England BN7 1XU
Distributed in Australia by Capricorn Link (Australia) Pty. Ltd.
P.O. Box 704, Windsor, NSW 2756, Australia

Sterling ISBN-13: 978-1-4027-2383-4
ISBN-10: 1-4027-2383-0

For information about custom editions, special sales, premium and
corporate purchases, please contact Sterling Special Sales
Department at 800-805-5489 or specialsales@sterlingpub.com.

Opposite: Fireworks over Manhattan.

Contents

Strolling Through New York's Favorite Neighborhoods . . .118

Off the Beaten Path: Outer Islands 146

Notes on Sources

This book is entirely indebted to a number of source materials. The esteemed *Encyclopedia of New York City*, edited by Kenneth T. Jackson (New Haven: Yale University Press, 1995), served as a main resource for information. In addition, Kevin Walsh's website *Forgotten New York*, http://www.forgotten-ny.com/ © 1999–2005. Midnight Fish, served as a critical resource for lesserknown historical sites and islands. Tom Fletcher's *new york architecture images and notes*, http://www.nyc-architecture.com/, was very helpful regarding architecture, and the film *New York: A Documentary Film*, directed by Ric Burns ["The American Experience", PBS] provided important insights for this author—particularly its final episode, "Center of the World". Finally, *Gotham: A History of New York City to 1898* (NY: Oxford University Press, 1998) by Edwin G. Burrows and Mike Wallace served as a major resource as well.

A number of government websites provided source material, including NYC Landmarks Preservation Commission, NYC Department of Parks and Recreation, NYC Department of Housing and Preservation, and the National Parks Service. In addition, several university and independent websites represent important sources for this work, including Paul Halsall, Fordham University, *Medieval New York Guide*, http://www.fordham.edu/halsall/med/medny.html; Graduate School of Journalism—Columbia University, *Beyond Manhattan, New York's Other Islands*, http://nyc24.jrn.columbia.edu/2003/islands/index.html, Kevin Matthews, and *Great Buildings Online*, http://www.greatbuildings.com/ © 1994–2006.

Finally, many of the institutions featured here—from Carnegie Hall to Grand Central Terminal to the Metropolitan Museum of Art—mount home pages which provided critical information to this book. Detailed and comprehensive, these websites are worth visiting for historical information and contemporary events alike.

Please note: NYC & Company is the official source of tourism statistics for the city. The research department develops and distributes information on NYC domestic and international visitor statistics and monitors the travel industry's impact on the city's economy.

This book would not have been completed without the help and inspiration of Karen Gillen, Louise Quayle, Megan DeMonte, and Isabel Sanchez.

Introduction:
Man, Mammon and Manhattan:
A History of the Big Apple

The best, most effective medicine my soul has yet partaken—the grandest physical habitat and surroundings of land and water the globe affords.

—poet Walt Whitman
regarding his 1878 visit to New York

New York City is an international city, a microcosm of the United States, and an icon in popular culture. In reality, it is simply a collection of many neighborhoods scattered

Evacuation of New York City by the British, November 25, 1783.

among five boroughs—Manhattan, Brooklyn, Queens, the Bronx, and Staten Island—but, as the saying goes, the whole is greater than the sum of its parts. In 2005, 6.8 million tourists from abroad visited New York, some of whom came to see their friends and relatives. More than 400 years after the first European exploration of this land located at the mouth of the Hudson River, New York remains a magnet for immigrants not only from Europe, but from the entire planet. The U.S. Census Bureau stated in 2003 that 35.9 percent of New York City's 8.1 million residents had been born outside the U.S. New York is the most ethnically diverse, religiously varied urban center in the country. Each one of New York's neighborhoods has its own rhythm and lifestyle, and moving from one neighborhood to another may seem like traveling from one country to another. No other U.S. city has contributed more images to the collective consciousness of Americans. Wall Street means finance, Broadway is synonymous with theater, Fifth Avenue is associated with shopping, Madison Avenue means the advertising industry, Greenwich Village connotes bohemian lifestyles, Seventh Avenue signifies fashion, Tammany Hall defines machine politics, and Harlem evokes images of the Jazz Age and the nexus of African-American culture. New York City's preeminent symbol is the Statue of Liberty, but the metropolis is itself an icon, the arena in which Emma Lazarus's "tempest-tost" people of every nation are transformed into Americans—and if they remain in the city, they become New Yorkers. For the past two centuries, New York has been the largest and wealthiest American city. More than half the people and goods that ever entered the United States came through its port, and that stream of commerce has made change a constant presence in city life.

NEW YORK CITY.—OUR INDIAN ALLIES.—SIOUX WARRIORS MAKING PURCHASES ON BROADWAY FOR THEMSELVES AND SQUAWS, OCTOBER 5TH.—SEE PAGE 107.

BURIAL OF GENERAL CUSTER'S REMAINS.

THE remains of the gallant General Custer were recovered from the bloody field where he fell, ... were found at the extreme end and highest point of a broken, treeless ridge. Close by lay his brother, Colonel Thomas Custer, and other officers and friends, surrounded by the partially exposed and bleaching bones of the soldiers and their horses, ... dently been disfigured by the coyotes or savages, and probably both, and many, if not the most, of the skulls there and throughout all the fields were smashed to fragments, mangled or missing, still what was decided to be and probably were the main portions of the bones of General Custer and ... remains were carefully gathered, wrapped and then packed with grass cut from Custer's Valley, placed in ten rough boxes not unlike rough coffins, and brought away.

By request of his father, the gallant Lieutenant Crittenden sleeps where he fell, with his boys about ...

Native Americans examining goods inside a shop on Broadway, 1877.

Four centuries ago, New York City was populated by Native Americans who farmed the land and lived off the Atlantic Ocean, The Hudson River, and the small canals weaving their way through this coastal part of the North American mainland.

The first known explorer to reach the area was Italy's Giovanni da Verrazano, sent in the 1520s by Francis I of France to find a direct sailing route to the resource-rich Pacific. However, it was not until 1624 that modern-day New York formally began as a Dutch settlement. The early explorers who opened these territories to European expansion, adventurers such as da Verrazano and England's Henry Hudson, are well remembered in popular historical accounts. They have been commemorated in the names of the waterways that gave them access to these shorelines. In the case of da Verrazano, the bridge connecting Staten Island and Brooklyn was named after him.

Dutch names have also left an imprint throughout the city, although the language has not been in daily usage for approximately two hundred years. Brooklyn was originally called Breukelen, and Harlem and Staten Island were spelled "Haarlem" and "Staten Eylandt," respectively. In fact, New Yorkers use Dutch words every day without realizing it. They eat "cookies" and "crullers," they carry a "knapsack" to school, or schedule a meeting with the "boss." The two most common types of words from Dutch are seafaring and painting terms. Sailors still say "ahoy" as a nautical greeting and "avast" as a term for "stop". They refer to the "boom" of a ship, take orders from the "skipper," and they "hoist" a sail and "dock" a ship. If the sailors win the "lottery," they may buy a "yacht." Meanwhile on dry land,

Above: Inauguration of the Bartholdi statue. The Statue of Liberty is partly clouded by smoke from a military and naval salute marking the president's arrival, October 28, 1886.

Below: Grant's Tomb dedication, circa 1897.

City Hall, circa 1900.

artists work with an "easel" and "etch" an engraving.

The area's Native American past is also remembered in some of the city's modern-day names. Several locations in the metropolitan area echo New York's precolonial history. Some even say, for instance, that the name Manhattan stands as a derivative of the Indian word *menatay*, or "island". Old paths once used by indigenous people retain their active presence in today's cartography. The Bowery, for example, is a street representing a vestige of an old Indian route through the length of Manhattan. Likewise, Broadway began as an old Algonquin trade route called the Wiechquaekeck trail.

Lenape means "men" or "people" in Munsee, the dialect spoken by the first New Yorkers, who called the area Lenapehoking, or "place where the Lenape live." They were Algonquins, not Iroquois, as is commonly thought. Estimates are that, at the time of the Dutch settlers' arrival, approximately 15,000 Native Americans lived in the area which is now called New York City. Unfortunately, there are no remaining Lenape communities in twenty-first-century New York.

Despite the early dominance of the Dutch, New York's seventeenth-century population was richly diverse. The area counted Protestant Walloons, Brazilian Jews, French Huguenots, Germans, English, French, Swedes, and Africans, among others.

Africans had an important history in the colony as they had been transported to the new world as slaves. The port of Nieuw Amsterdam

Construction of the Flatiron Building, circa 1902.

became embroiled in the American Revolutionary War.

Although New York State was home to the Battle of Long Island and patriots like James Duane and John Jay, it was occupied by Tory loyalists during the war, extending its British legacy longer than that of other early colonies. After independence, from 1789 to 1790, New York served briefly as the capital of the new nation. During this period, the first president of the U.S., General George Washington, was inaugurated on the steps of Federal Hall in downtown Manhattan. A high-profile character, Washington frequented such places as St. Paul's Chapel, an early chapel of Trinity Church. Washington is commemorated throughout the city, from a sculpture in City Hall to the arch in Washington Square Park to the statue in Union Square.

Although New York has played a major role in U.S. political history, the city has distinguished itself as the nation's capital of commerce, not of politics. Understanding New York's relationship to commerce is central to understanding the history of the city.

At the end of the eighteenth and start of the nineteenth centuries, an industrialized New York emerged well positioned between Europe and the agricultural economy of the South. Its role as a financial center took on greater importance. One example is the formation of the New York Stock Exchange (NYSE) in 1792, although securities trading did not become popular until the end of the War of 1812.

Economic expansion mushroomed after the 1811 passage of the Commissioners' Plan, creating a grid map of streets and allotting space for the creation of new buildings. The construction of the Erie Canal in 1825 only added to the prominent role New York played in the growing

served as an important slave-trading station for the Dutch West India Company, although some slaves were later freed. By the time of the Revolutionary War, nearly 15 percent of New Yorkers were black, most of whom were slaves or former slaves. The practice of racial slavery was finally abolished in New York in 1827.

The city took on its present name in 1667, after Charles II of England renamed the territory in honor of his brother, James Duke of York, who was in charge of the British Royal Navy. As a crucial seaport in the British Empire, New York's fate was strongly influenced by Britain's fortunes. As a result, the colony eventually economy. The Erie Canal linked New York Harbor to inland lakes, creating an expanded trade route between the metropolis and other parts of the U.S.

By the middle of the nineteenth century, the city housed a high concentration of merchants, traders, small shop owners, farmers, and laborers that sustained its residential life. Capital, goods, and people flowed in and out of New York, transforming the city into one of the busiest ports in the nation. Nineteenth-century New York became the heart of the nation's industrial and commercial empire.

New York's floodtide of immigrants and the ensuing supply of cheap labor played an integral part of its role as a port and center for commerce. During the second half of the nine-

teenth century, the city's population exploded. Many of these new residents were recent immigrants from Europe who fled their homelands to escape poverty or religious persecution. Although not alone as a port in the history of U.S. immigration, New York was a major entry point into the U.S. for millions of people. By the end of the nineteenth century, many of the immigrants who came to these shores chose to settle in the city and its surrounding areas. At the beginning of the twenty-first century, New York housed immigrants from more than 180 countries.

Manhattan and the outlying boroughs of Brooklyn, Queens, the Bronx and Staten Island were consolidated into one city in 1898. According to its proponents, centralized govern-

Jakob Mittelstadt and family, May 9, 1905. Admitted to go to Kullen, North Dakota. Photographed by A.F. Sherman, circa 1905.

ment and unification of the area surrounding the New York Harbor would benefit the economic, political, and cultural life of the region.

New York in the nineteenth century, while primarily under the control of the Tammany Hall political machine, constructed Manhattan's basic water, sewer, fire, police, transportation, and park facilities. In 1899 social reformer Jacob Riis described a metropolis "barely yet out of its knickerbockers" yet poised for greatness; Riis believed its enduring challenge would be to care for the poor.

A step towards caring for the poor was the establishment of public and private school systems. In the 1840s, Roman Catholic Archbishop John Hughes was instrumental in establishing a Catholic parochial school system. Neither the public or parochial systems ever achieved universal attendance during the nineteenth century, although in

1874 a compulsory attendance law for the primary grades was enacted. After consolidation of the five boroughs, Greater New York launched a massive public building program to provide schools where a half-million eligible students could be educated each year. Secondary education was not even offered to its children until the late nineteenth century, but by 1920 construction made primary education, along with both ordinary and specialized high schools, available for everyone.

By the beginning of the twentieth century, New York was the headquarters for more than two-thirds of the top 100 American corporations, and its 25,000 factories manufactured several hundred different industrial products. It led the nation in total factory workers, number of factories, capital valuation, and product value. New York held its leadership position for another three generations and provided nearly one

Suffragettes, preceded by policemen, leaving City Hall, October 28, 1908.

Newspaper vendors on Park Row, by L. W. Hine, July 1910.

million industrial jobs into the 1950s. In 1960–75 the city lost more than 600,000 of these jobs, as its old economy collapsed and an information age took shape. Banking and financial services became the new engine of development—abetted by the traditional print and advertising sectors of the economy—while white-collar workers with computer skills added to the diverse labor pool of the city. Although much clothing production has moved out of New York, it remains the city's leading industry, and sweatshop conditions reminiscent of the early 1900s still exist in small factories throughout the five boroughs.

The 1970s represented a low point for New York; its national reputation collapsed as the government experienced virtual bankruptcy. High rents, congestion, arson, and crime led to an exodus by businesses and the middle class even after the city began the rebuilding process. Industrial parks, where businesses were given cheaper rents, better utilities, and safety, were

authorized in response to the crisis, and major tax incentives were granted to those corporations that remained in the city. The New York Stock Exchange even threatened to leave, but in the late 1990s it agreed to remain in Manhattan and to construct a new facility. New York marketed its monetary expertise to the globe; its banks dealt with the Latin American debt crisis of the 1980s as well as the Asian financial meltdown of the late 1990s, and in the process the city became the "economic capital of the world." The metropolitan area is home to more than one-fifth of the Fortune 500 companies.

The twenty-first century began with the tragic attack on the World Trade Center in 2001. The tragedy of September 11, 2001, painfully reminded residents of the fragility of human life. New Yorkers' image as brusque was shattered as thousands of mourners gathered on every corner of the city in the days that followed. Tributes in Union Square drew city residents from every socioeconomic group. They attended memorial

Wall Street, by I. Underhill, circa 1911.

services, reflected in quiet contemplation, and shared their pain. The names of the victims of the attack are commemorated in the Union Square subway station display measuring 4 feet high and 50 feet across.

Movers and Shakers: New York's Transportation and Industry

The inhabitants of New York are the most locomotive people on the face of the earth.
—James Boardman, 1830

From every angle, the city's infrastructure commands attention. Its bridges, subway lines, business centers and squares—the foundations of its transportation, communication and commercial lines—knit together its disparate islands and neighborhoods. Today the city enjoys 578 miles of waterfront, and the New York City

Department of Transportation operates 750 bridge structures and tunnels. Public transportation on the Metropolitan Transit Authority's buses and subway trains runs 24 hours a day, 7 days a week, contributing to the feeling that New York is a "city that never sleeps."

Throughout the first half of the twentieth century, the city became a world center for industry, commerce, and communication. Interborough Rapid Transit (the first subway company) began operating in 1904, and the railroads operating out of Grand Central Terminal thrived. The city is home, of course, to a number of famous bridges; the Williamsburg, Manhattan, and George Washington bridges have earned notable spots in the skyline. The Brooklyn Bridge is perhaps the city's most famous and beautiful bridge, and its pedestrian walkway with romantic views of Manhattan and Brooklyn remains a favorite destination with tourists and residents alike.

The entertainment industry has taken New York to its heart. In 2004, more than 90 television shows and hundreds of films were shot on location in New York City. Today there are more than 40 studios and soundstages in Manhattan, Brooklyn, Queens, and the Bronx. As many of the locations used in films and television are on the street, visitors can see famed locations like the apartment where the Friends lived, the diner where Jerry Seinfeld ate, and the brownstone where Bill Cosby's family lived. While some consider New York's commerce and transportation to be the body of the city, others believe the parks are its soul.

On the Sunny Side of the Street: Parks and Other Outdoor Spaces

The skyline of New York is a monument of a splendour that no pyramids or palaces will ever equal or approach.
— Novelist Ayn Rand

While the eye is inevitably drawn upwards to the city's tall buildings, the horizon of New York is also filled with lovely parks and outdoor spaces to enjoy. A large part of the credit goes to park czar Robert Moses, who held various New York State government positions, including head of park commissions, for about 40 years. His career

Coney Island, no date recorded.

in public works planning resulted in a virtual transformation of the New York landscape. Among the works completed under his supervision were a network of 35 highways, 12 bridges, numerous parks, the Lincoln Center for the Performing Arts, Shea Stadium, many housing projects, and the 1964 New York World's Fair. His projects greatly influenced large-scale planning in other cities. He was also instrumental in bringing the United Nations complex to Manhattan's East River waterfront.

Since Moses retired about 40 years ago, New York has continued to expand its parks system. One of the most highly anticipated projects is the completion of Hudson River Park, which will extend along the Manhattan's West Side water-

front from 59th Street to Chambers Street. The park encompasses 550 acres, including 400 acres of open water that will provide an exciting public venue for boating, touring, fishing, swimming, and many other activities. The heart of the park will be 13 old maritime piers that are being reconstructed as public park spaces. These piers will include lawns and gardens, picnic areas, scenic overlooks, playgrounds, ball fields, volleyball courts, community docks, historic boats, a living museum, research and educational facilities, event space, places to eat, and much more. The Greenwich Village section of the park was completed and opened to the public in May 2003; Clinton Cove Park at 54th Street opened in May 2005, and much of the rest of the Clinton

Horse-drawn carriages in Central Park, no date recorded.

GREENWICH VILLAGE FAIR • "HOT DOGS"   4212-6

Greenwich Village fair, no date recorded.

section of the park is expected to open by the spring of 2007. In total, the city boasts over 1,700 parks, playgrounds, and recreational facilities across the five boroughs.

Landmarks: Temples of Worship, Commerce, and Sport

This city is esteemed the most eligible situation for commerce in the United States.
—John Payne, *Universal Geography*, 1799

New York City had an estimated gross metropolitan product of $488.8 billion in 2003. If it were a nation, the city would have the sixteenth highest gross domestic product in the world, exceeding that of Russia ($433 billion). Commercial banking began in Manhattan in 1784 when the Bank of New York opened for business. It was soon joined by a branch of the First Bank of the United States (1792) and the Manhattan Company (1799), ancestor of what is now the Chase Manhattan Corporation. The origins of the New York Stock Exchange (NYSE) can be traced to the Buttonwood Agreement of 1792, although the Exchange Board itself was not organized until 1817. After the Erie Canal opened, banking services became even more centered in the city, and when its merchants entered the cotton trade the commerce of the entire nation flowed into the port. Several financial panics in the nineteenth century could not prevent the city from dominating the national money markets. Investors and banks from the metropolis provided much of the capital that financed the industrialization of the country. So great was the influence of New York that the country's largest firms found it expedient to locate their headquarters there even though—as with Carnegie Steel, American Tobacco, and Standard Oil—the focus of their manufacturing was elsewhere.

While high finance became a major part of the city's economy, the tourism industry also blossomed. Visitors in search of an once-in-a-lifetime experience ended up at the Plaza Hotel (1907) on 5th Avenue opposite Central Park. It soon became the premier place in the city for romantic, festive gatherings. Lavish weddings were performed; newlywed couples celebrated their wedding night; young singletons went to Trader Vic's to eat brunch and meet old college friends; little girls got dressed up in their finery to sip tea with their grandmothers and listen to a string quartet in the Palm Court; out-of-town tourists saved money for months to spend a long weekend in the elegant, landmark structure. Although other elegant lodgings were available, the Plaza became New York's most beloved hotel. Even schoolchildren who had never visited the city daydreamed of wandering its hallways following the publication of the classic children's book *Eloise*.

Skyscrapers, those cathedrals of business, serve as a reminder that the flow of capital steers the course of the city's future, and are iconic structures associated with New York's image. The Woolworth Building, for example, was instantly dubbed the "cathedral of commerce" for its Gothic design in service of industry. Skyscrapers have always fascinated New Yorkers, and their height, novelty, and grace have attracted the attention of artists and photographers.

While faith in the future of capitalism is embodied in the continued construction of skyscrapers, religious faith is also well represented in the city. Every major religious group has a presence in New York, from Gothic cathedrals in uptown Manhattan to storefront Buddhist temples in Chinatown.

Fifth Avenue, December 18, 1913.

Reception of Prince of Udine passing through Washington Arch, 1917.

Cultural Capital of the United States: Broadway, Museums and Universities

New York, the nation's thyroid gland.
—Christopher Morley

Why is New York called the Big Apple? In the 1920s, a sportswriter for the *Morning Telegraph* named John Fitzgerald overheard stable hands in New Orleans refer to New York City's racetracks as "the Big Apple." He named his column "Around the Big Apple." A decade later, jazz musicians adopted the term to refer to New York City, and especially Harlem, as the jazz capital of the world. There are many apples on the trees of success, they said, but when one picks New York City, one picks the big apple. Many people from all over the United States are attracted to New York City for its culture, energy, cosmopolitanism, and by their own hope of making it big in the "Big Apple."

New York has long drawn artists with its dazzling nightlife and vibrant cultural scene. The city is known for its museums and has hundreds of them. Many are world-renowned, like the Metropolitan Museum of Art, the Whitney Museum of American Art, and the Solomon R. Guggenheim Museum. The famed Museum Mile stretches from 82nd Street to 102nd Street along Fifth Avenue and contains several world-famous museums. In other parts of the city, one can find collected artwork in some unlikely places, such as the murals of Stuart Davis in Radio City Music Hall and sculptures based on Pablo Picasso's work writ large on the campus of New York University.

Brooklyn Bridge and Brooklyn, by I. Underhill, circa 1919.

As a magnet for education, New York attracts students from all over the U.S. and dozens of countries. The metropolitan area has more than 80 colleges, including such nationally famed institutions as Columbia (founded 1754), New York (1831), Fordham (1841), and Rockefeller (1901) universities and the Cooper Union (1859). Its vast municipal system, the City University of New York (CUNY), has more than 20 units and traces its origin to City College (1847).

Strolling Through New York's Favorite Neighborhoods

It'll be a great place if they ever finish it.
—Attributed to author O. Henry

Walking is not only an efficient way to navigate congested New York byways, but a highly enjoy-able way to view the 6,375 miles (10,200 km) of streets. Manhattan is the smallest, oldest, densest, and most affluent borough. It has some of the oldest streets, structures, and neighborhoods. New York City's hundreds of neighborhoods remain the heart of the city. Of course, many neighborhoods were originally seafaring or farm-land communities. And those areas on the periphery remained rural longer than the core of the city. In the outer boroughs, neighborhoods began as small cities or towns. Brooklyn, for its part, remains the most populous borough. It was once the nation's third-largest city. The mansions of the once–resort town of Bay Ridge and aban-doned warehouses off the wharves of Huron in once-industrial Greenpoint reveal something of its diverse historic character.

Greenwich Village has had several transfor-mations, from its founding in the seventeenth century through its role as a posh suburb in the nineteenth century to its eventual fame in the twentieth century as America's "Left Bank." Greenwich Village has long been known for its tolerant and bohemian attitudes.

The Bronx is the only borough connected to the continental mainland of the U.S. It was settled in 1639 and it is named for the Swedish settler, Jonas Bronck. It was known colloquially as the Bronck's farm, and later shortened to the Bronck's. The name was Anglicized, and "the" became an inseparable part of the name. There are more than 60 landmarks and historic districts in the Bronx, including the Edgar Allen Poe Cottage on the Grand Concourse and the stately Van Cortlandt House Museum in Van Cortlandt Park.

Some New Yorkers believe that each street, even each city block, has its own character.

However, certain crossroads took on added importance over time. One of the most important crossroads in the history of the city no longer exists. The Five Points neighborhood was demolished in the 1890s, first to make way for a park, and then as the spot for many of the city's civic buildings. Named for the points created by the intersection of Park, Worth, and Baxter streets, the neighborhood was known as a center of vice and debauchery throughout the nineteenth century. Director Martin Scorsese depicted a fictionalized account of the neighborhood in his film *Gangs of New York*.

In the 1980s, an ancient African-American burial ground was discovered during construction of a government office tower in lower Manhattan. Slaves' remains and some of their possessions were unearthed and moved to forensic centers for further study. Part of the area

Times Square on Broadway and 44th Street, by International News Service photographer, 1929.

Empire State Building under construction, by L. W. Hine, 1931.

that had been designated for the office tower was instead preserved as a tribute to the unknown African-Americans whose labor played an indispensable role in building the city.

Off the Beaten Path: Outer Islands

> *Give me your tired, your poor,*
> *Your huddled masses yearning to breathe free,*
> *The wretched refuse of your teeming shore.*
> *Send these, the homeless, tempest-tost to me,*
> *I lift my lamp beside the golden door!*
> —Inscription on the Statue of Liberty, from
> Emma Lazarus's poem "The New Colossus"

The poet Emma Lazarus, descendant of an old New York Jewish family and long active in Jewish philanthropy in the city, wrote her famous poem to the Statue of Liberty, "The New Colossus," for the benefit of the American campaign to raise funds for the base of the statue. It was first read at the National Academy of Design on December 3, 1883, and twenty years later it was inscribed in bronze on the pedestal.

Liberty Island, home of the Statue of Liberty, is the most famous in the city, which is comprised of an archipelago of islands. It is only a few minutes by ferry from Liberty Island to Ellis Island. Between 1892 and 1924, 12 million immigrants passed through Ellis Island; two-thirds of them went immediately to Manhattan's Lower East Side. Some stayed just a few weeks before moving on; others settled and became a part of the fabric of New York City. Some of the immigrants who passed through Ellis Island and went on to illustrious careers are: Irving Berlin, musician, arrived in 1893 from Russia; Marcus Garvey, politician, arrived 1916 from Jamaica; Bob Hope, comedian, arrived in 1908 from England; Knute Rockne, football coach, arrived in 1893 from Norway; and the von Trapp family of *Sound of Music* fame, arrived in 1938 from Austria.

Other, smaller islands such as City Island and Roosevelt Island are not only physically separated from the five boroughs but maintain unique identities. City Island has a proud history of boatbuilding and sea fishing, and its mouthwatering seafood restaurants attract diners from the tristate area. This island is part of the Bronx, but it feels like a New England fishing village, offering marinas with fishing and boating. Roosevelt Island is a middle-class housing project that feels like small-town America while enjoying spectacular views of the Manhattan skyline. One of the most famous islands, Coney Island, is no longer an island but a peninsula attached to Brooklyn as a result of landfill. After having more ups and downs than the Cyclone roller coaster, an historic landmark in Coney Island, the neighborhood enjoyed a revival in the first decade of the twenty-first century, and New Yorkers looking for a cheap, fun day out in the city flock to its amusement park rides.

What is it about New York that captures the imagination of the nation, and perhaps the world? Is it the history? Politics? Finance? Culture? Character? Yes, it is these things and more. A tour of New York reveals a fascinating story at every street corner. Every New Yorker has a dream; everyone considers himself or herself a star; everyone is on the move. Even in the aftermath of September 11, New York continues to be a city of hope where the American dream thrives.

View from Empire State Building to Chrysler Building and Queensboro Bridge, by S. H. Gottscho, January 19, 1932.

Movers and Shakers:
New York's Transportation
and Industry

Above: View of Brooklyn Bridge from Brooklyn Park.

Opposite: Crossing the Brooklyn Bridge.

Brooklyn Bridge

The Brooklyn Bridge—a favorite pedestrian and traffic crossing memorialized in films, songs, and poems—was the first steel suspension bridge to link Brooklyn to the island of Manhattan. It is the work of German-born John Augustus Roebling.

At the time of its construction, Brooklyn was far more rural than its urban neighbor to the west. Some thought that connecting these two boroughs represented a wise solution to overcrowding problems in Manhattan. Work began on the bridge near the end of the 1860s, but construction was delayed by the sudden death of Roebling from tetanus. Soon after the tragedy, work was taken up by his son, Washington Roebling, from his Columbia Heights home.

The bridge features several engineering innovations. Builders used steel, an uncommon material for the time. For stability, the bridge's towers needed to sit on bedrock. Some of the bedrock rested on shore, but much of it lay far below the water. As a result, airtight cylinders or "caissons" were constructed, floated out, and sunk into the East River. Submerged in the treacherous working conditions of these underwater cylinders, many of the men who dug into the riverbed died of "caissons disease," also called "the bends."

The Brooklyn Bridge was opened on May 24, 1883, with the longest span in the world at that time. It became an immediate icon, a symbol of the city, of urbanism, and of the power of engineering. As a result, it garnered praise and disdain from all quarters. Although Henry James criticized the structure, Walt Whitman and Joseph Stella penned and painted unadulterated praise.

According to some statistics, the Brooklyn Bridge is the second-busiest bridge in New York City. After more than 100 years, the bridge's span still ranks forty-fourth among the world's suspension bridges.

Previous page: New York water taxi, South Street Seaport.

Grand Central Terminal

The early rail lines into New York City—the New York, Harlem, New Haven, and Hudson railroads—were built in the middle of the nineteenth century. Soon, the expanding web of track, terminals, and passenger stations generated an eclectic and often confusing mix of traffic. City streets saw a combination of rail, horse-drawn, and steam-powered vehicles. To the contemporary eye, the blend seems quaintly chaotic. This dense and varied constellation created real problems for the citizenry. Pollution, traffic, and accidents plagued the metropolis. Steam locomotives, in particular, were extremely noisy and they were soon denied service south of 42nd Street. All of these stresses compelled the creation of a centralized terminal.

Today's Grand Central was born of shipping magnate "Commodore" Cornelius Vanderbilt. By 1869, he owned all the rail lines into the city. Vanderbilt hired John B. Snook to design a main depot that would consolidate rail traffic. Called Grand Central Depot, the building was located on 42nd Street and 4th Avenue.

It soon became clear, however, that the facility did not meet the needs of New Yorkers. It failed to eliminate noise and air pollution. Its safety was called into question after a major train collision. Public demand led to an increase in the number of electric trains and underground tunnels.

In 1903, several architectural firms were invited to submit designs for the new Grand Central Terminal. McKim, Mead, and White were among the prominent firms asked to compete. The concession was won by lesser-known Reed and Stem Engineering. Reed and Stem, in conjunction with Whitney Warren, who worked on the façade on 42nd Street, collaborated to create the present-day Grand Central Terminal. The building's majesty is undeniable. It holds fascinating details within the coves of its splendor. Statues of Hermes, Minerva, Mercury, and Hercules gesture in tribute to the powerful combination of transportation and commerce.

The new Grand Central Terminal opened in 1913. A large space, its main concourse is 118 feet

(36 meters) wide, 374 feet (114 meters) long, and 125 feet (38 meters) high. More than 140,000 commuters rush through this enchanting, eclectic and busy space every day.

Because of its midtown location in a prospering neighborhood, it was often in jeopardy from urban development. To protect it from the wrecking ball, Grand Central was designated a landmark in the 1960s. Its new status, however, did not please the owners, who hoped to profit from future development. They filed a lawsuit against the City of New York in a litigation battle that lasted for nearly a decade. Many supporters fought for the terminal's preservation, including former First Lady Jacqueline Kennedy Onassis. In the end, landmark status was granted in December 1976 and was upheld by the U.S. Supreme Court on June 26, 1978.

Park Row

Along Park Row, in downtown Manhattan, sits the remains of Newspaper Row, New York's vibrant news capital during the early nineteenth century. Here, newspaper publishers built skyscrapers along the avenue because of its close proximity to City Hall and the financial district. Newspaper work brought all manner of business with it. They not only wrote the news here, but manufactured its equipment, advertised its product, and printed its pages. Park Row was home to the *New York Times*, the *Tribune*, and the *Recorder*, to name only a few. The "yellow journalism" wars between Joseph Pulitzer's New York World and William Randolph Hearst's New York Journal took place on its streets.

Architectural relics of this dynamic era remain. They include the Potter Building (1883) at 38 Park Row, which contained the headquarters of the *New York Press*. A stunning twin-domed building sitting at 15 Park Row (1896–99) was briefly the tallest building in Manhattan, and once housed the offices of the Associated Press. George B. Post's New York Times Building (1889) once stood at 41 Park Row.

At the turn of the twentieth century, the papers began to move uptown. The *New York Times* relocated to Long Acre Square, which was renamed Times Square in its honor. By 1920, Newspaper Row ceased to serve as the central place for the news business. Over half of Newspaper Row was demolished in later years. The entrance ramp to the Brooklyn Bridge played a role in toppling the Pulitzer Building in 1955. Pace University's massive tower replaced the Tribune Building in 1966.

Left: City Hall Park.

Opposite: Potter Building at 38 Park Row.

Rockefeller Center

Rockefeller Center is a commercial and entertainment complex located in the heart of midtown Manhattan on a piece of land previously known as the "speakeasy belt." John D. Rockefeller Jr. held a multimillion-dollar lease on the property and planned to revitalize the area. After the stock market crash, Rockefeller abandoned the idea of a cultural center and shifted his focus to a commercial one.

During the heart of the Depression, the proposition seemed grand, if not reckless. The promise of profitability was no easy task, but Rockefeller Center's design created an optimistic setting that belied the test of hard times. Its seductive slopes led pedestrians to benches, fountains and, of course, shops. Moreover, the plan called for a series of underground corridors that would link the subway directly to services—an ingenious commercial pull.

In addition to its shopping, Rockefeller Center is known for entertainment events. It also features a number of noteworthy sights, including a sunken plaza, outdoor ice-skating rink, and Paul Manship's eye-catching gilded statue, *Prometheus*. Lee

Rockefeller Plaza's statue Atlas *by Lee Lowrie and Rene Chambellan.*

Outdoor skating rink with Paul Manship's gilded statue of Prometheus.

Lowrie's limestone and glass sculpture *Wisdom, Light and Sound* marks the main entrance. Anecdotally, an original mural by Diego Rivera was commissioned, removed, and destroyed as a result of controversy between Rockefeller and Rivera regarding a painted figure that resembled Vladimir Lenin. Instead the mural work of Jose Maria Sert and Frank Brangwyn, titled *Man's Intellectual Mastery of the Material Universe* and *Man's Conquest of the Material World,* adorn the ceiling—a fitting title for Rockefeller's ambition.

Lore has it that laborers decorated the first Christmas tree on the site during the Depression. The tradition lives on. The giant spruce that graces the plaza has dazzling decorations. The lighting of the tree is a yearly event broadcast throughout the U.S. by the National Broadcasting Company, whose headquarters are located at 30 Rockefeller Plaza. With a glorious nod to the holiday spirit, thousands of tourists and even locals with their "seen-it-all" attitude jam the area every December.

South Street Seaport

Some date South Street Seaport back to 1600. The original shore road was called Pearl Street, named after its pearly oyster-shell casing. Sea captains chose the area because it provided shelter from the strong winds and ice that damaged ships navigating the Hudson River in the winter.

As the epicenter of the city's port life, the area was alight with business of all kinds—with import and export merchants, tackle shops, warehouses, and rooming houses. The seaport had its fair share of social institutions as well, from saloons and brothels to the evangelical organizations that preached against their dangers.

South Street Seaport served as a vital port of Manhattan for much of the nineteenth century. Toward the end of the century, steam replaced sail power. The water near its shore was too shallow to accommodate the hulls of the ocean-going vessels that dominated global port life. As a result, many shipping lines left for more welcoming posts along the Hudson River. Port life abandoned the once-thriving area, save for a couple of remaining shipping lines and the Fulton Fish Market. Gradually, South Street's dominance in the history of trade waned.

During the twentieth century, waterfront work on the old San Francisco port on the West Coast stirred restoration efforts here. The South Street Seaport Museum opened in 1967. In 1979, the area officially became an historic district, a move advocated by some of the same supporters for landmark designation of the Quincy Market District in Boston, Massachusetts. These supporters, with the help of city grant money, transformed the area into a vibrant complex of restored nineteenth-century buildings. Located on the waterfront with historic ships abutting a modern market place, the port draws the curious and commercially minded to its shores, much as it did hundreds of years ago.

Pilot House from a 1923 New York Central tugboat.

Times Square

"Celebrate New Year's Eve with 750,000 of your closest friends!" This invitation is issued every December by organizers of the event that draws thousands of spectators who jam the street, counting down the final seconds of the year in unison as the lighted ceremonial ball begins its descent at 11:59 p.m.

Times Square—the "crossroads of the world"—used to be called Long Acre Square, and in the nineteenth century it was filled with carriage-building shops and livery stables. The site was renamed Times Square after the *New York Times* moved its headquarters there in 1904. It evolved into a commercial and entertainment center as theaters relocated from the Bowery.

Revelers began celebrating New Year's Eve in Times Square as early as 1904, but it was in 1907 that the New Year's Eve ball made its maiden descent from the flagpole atop One Times Square.

The ball has been lowered every year except in 1942 and 1943, when its use was suspended due to the World War II "dim out" of lights in the city. Crowds still gathered in Times Square and greeted the New Year with a moment of silence followed by chimes ringing out from One Times Square.

After the 1929 stock market crash, the area underwent radical change. Plagued by the same economic woes that blanketed the nation, the neighborhood suffered a slow but steady decline that continued through the 1980s. After a late twentieth-century makeover, Times Square has been revitalized as a major tourist attraction as well as a cultural and commercial center.

Left: Equestrian statue of George Washington, created by Henry Kirke Brown and unveiled in 1856.

Union Square

One of the city's nearly forty squares, Union Square has long been an important site of public life in the city, a gathering place for recreation and political expression.

At once surrounded by stylish buildings, concert halls and hotels, it was also a place where workers rallied and protested. Indeed, its environs served as the headquarters for a number of political parties, unions, and progressive organizations. The Democratic Party's political machine, which played a major role in local politics from the 1790s to the 1860s, made its home in Tammany Hall. Today, the building houses the New York Film Academy.

Frederick Law Olmsted and Calvert Vaux redesigned the park in 1871. Although much of their work was demolished by the construction of subway lines, below, their design was instrumental in the city's first Labor Day celebration in 1882.

During the 1980s, the city began to refurbish the park, and it was designated a national historic landmark in 1998. As commuters rush seven days a week to the large subway station, visitors with leisure time relax in the picnic areas, sit on the newly seeded lawns, or shop in the farmer's market. The streets opposite the park reemerged in the 1990s as a major shopping center following the area's decline 40 years previously when several large department stores moved or went out of business.

Greenmarket Farmers Market on Union Square, where regional growers sell their goods, is one of forty markets in the five boroughs, over half in Manhattan alone.

Verrazano-Narrows Bridge

Outside New York City, the Verrazano-Narrows Bridge is best known as the starting line for the New York City Marathon, a yearly event that attracts thousands of international participants and spectators every autumn. But New Yorkers know it best as the fastest way to travel between Staten Island and Brooklyn.

For many years after its completion in 1964, the Verrazano-Narrows had the longest span in the world, surpassed only by the Humber Bridge in England in 1981. To accommodate the bridge's length of 4,260 feet (1,298.4 meters), the towers are purposefully misaligned to fit the curvature of the earth.

The Verrazano-Narrows Bridge was designed by Swiss engineer Othmar H. Ammann and champi-

oned by Robert Moses. An ambitious urban planner, Moses took great pride in one of his last major public works projects in New York City; he famously called the bridge a "triumph of simplicity and restraint." Its long and straightforward form earns the accolade. Aesthetics and engineering aside, the Verrazano-Narrows Bridge accelerated the economic development of both Brooklyn and Staten Island, and became a major feature of the New York skyline. The ends of the bridge are located at historic Fort Hamilton in Brooklyn and Fort Wadsworth in Staten Island, two fortifications that guarded New York Harbor at the Narrows for over a century. The bridge was named after Giovanni da Verrazano, who, in 1524, was the first European explorer to sail into New York Harbor.

Wall Street

During the 1650s, the Dutch built a wall to protect lower Manhattan from incursion. Never used in battle, the wall was dismantled by the British, but the street that ran alongside it remained. Wall Street is the result.

Wall Street is best known as the site for the New York Stock Exchange, founded in 1817. The building was designed by George B. Post and completed in 1903.

The stock exchange began as a small call market with stock names shouted out as brokers tendered securities. At first, it traded only small volumes of shares. Despite millions spent on technology to handle its high volume, the NYSE remains a face-to-face trade setting. In the end, Wall Street is less the name of a street than an iconic reference to the chief engine of American capitalism.

The Wall Street area is also known for places like Fraunces Tavern at 54 Pearl Street, site of the infamous Fuerzas Armadas Liberacion Nacional Puertoriquena (the Puerto Rican independence movement known as FALN) bombing of 1975, and the site where George Washington bade farewell to his troops nearly two hundred years earlier.

Also noteworthy is Federal Hall, located at 26 Wall Street, which was the first capitol of the U.S. The original building was demolished in the nineteenth century and replaced by the current structure, the first U.S. Customs House. J.Q.A. Ward's statue of George Washington stands in front of the building, on the site where Washington was inaugurated as the first U.S. president.

New York Stock Exchange.

The Subway

With an average weekday ridership of 4.8 million people, the New York City subway system spans over 700 miles of track reaching 490 stations above and below ground. In terms of passenger traffic, New York's subway system ranks as the fifth largest in the world.

Although funds to build the subway were approved in 1894, builders faced challenges from the start. Workers had to circumvent underground streams and other obstacles to carefully navigate the world below the city streets—and some lost their lives in the process. The subway lines opened in 1904. With their web-like reach, they spurred growth in the city above.

In the 1970s, the subway system fell into decline. Some considered the ubiquitous mark of graffiti as representative of its fall, but others saw it as a burgeoning art form in its own right, creating a renaissance in underground art. During the 1980s and 1990s, extensive renovation and government investment sparked an increase in ridership.

Train buffs will enjoy a visit the New York Transit Museum in Brooklyn Heights. The museum is a surprising and edifying find for those who visit. Sculptures, mosaics, and quotations fill cab and tunnel walls. Most stations tie the artwork below to the neighborhoods in which they are located.

Times Square subway station.

The Staten Island Ferry

The Staten Island Ferry has become an iconic trip for tourists, particularly at night when the lights of the city are best seen from afar.

The ferry service was created for commuters to get to work in "the city," as residents of Staten Island, Brooklyn, Queens, and the Bronx are apt to call Manhattan.

Prices have hardly changed since the service originated in the late 1900s. The 5-cent fare was established 1897. In 1972, the fare was raised to 10 cents. In 1975, the fare was increased to 25 cents. In 1990, the fare went up to 50 cents. Finally on July 4, 1997, the fare for foot passengers on the ferry was eliminated, creating the most famous free ride in the city.

Three new ferries have been put into service in phases since 2005 at a cost of $40 million each. These ferries each carry 4,440 passengers and 30 vehicles. One of the design goals was to capture the "old style" ferry appearance and ambiance. As in the old car boats that had been in service previously, there are outside seating areas. There is also a seating area on the hurricane deck between the pilot houses. These new ferries have been designed to accept handicapped passengers.

World Trade Center

The World Trade Center was the result of an ambitious development project. Businessman David Rockefeller had long hoped to revitalize Lower Manhattan. When older brother Nelson was sworn in as Governor of New York, the two worked together to bring the project to fruition.

Like most development projects in the city, the center displaced previous residents and structures. The World Trade Center erased Radio Row from the map. As development on the World Trade Center progressed, protests raged against the real and symbolic changes that such a large-scale project would demand.

Construction was extremely complex, as builders had to dig deep below the man-made landfill to hit bedrock, while keeping out the Hudson River. The solution, "bathtub engineering," was innovative, as were the experimental designs to help the towers reach their great heights. At ground level, with a war raging and America's economic forecast sinking steadily into recession, not everyone appreciated these feats of engineering. A sign of the times, progress on the towers was slowed when scores of construction workers fought with antiwar demonstrators on the streets of Lower Manhattan in the early 1970s.

Construction continued despite tensions below. The World Trade Center consisted of seven buildings with two towers. Indeed, Architect Minoru Yamasaki's "Twin Towers," as they were called, were among the plan's most striking elements. In 1971, the first of the towers was topped off. So vast were the buildings they that had their own zip code. They were gigantic, like nothing else in the skyline, and their large size evoked criticism. According to lore, when tightrope walker Philippe Petit famously softened the hearts of New Yorkers on the morning of August 7, 1974, by walking between the two towers, locals began to see the Twin Towers as their own. In 1975, the observation deck on top of the South Tower was opened to the public for the first time, and it soon became one of the most popular tourist attractions in the city.

The Twin Towers stood 110 stories high and some say they swayed to the mercurial rhythm of the wind. Their height was a potent symbol of the city, modernity, and capitalism. By the 1990s, it became clear that terrorists had designated them as targets. In 1993, a bomb exploded in an underground parking garage killing five persons and wounding hundreds more. On the morning of September 11, 2001, two planes hit the Twin Towers in succession. The buildings collapsed to the ground. Government estimates of the total number of deaths have been adjusted several times; by 2003, the number stood at 2,752. The shock was felt across the globe. The event transformed the city, nation, and world. Immediate plans for redevelopment on the site reveal the respectful but forward-looking spirit of New Yorkers, showing the world something of the vitality that makes New York a potent symbol of progress.

Twin Towers of Light Memorial behind Statue of Liberty.

On the Sunny Side of
the Street: Parks and Other
Outdoor Spaces

Gramercy Park

According to historians, the Dutch called the Gramercy Park area Krom Moerasje, or "Little Crooked Swamp". The English changed the name to Gramercy. Present-day Gramercy Park can trace its start to 1831, when Sam Ruggles bought the property. He drained the swamp, planted trees and flowers, and arranged the streets around a private garden, all efforts to attract sales.

The Park's sixty-six lots went up for sale. Despite its horticultural display, many New Yorkers did not want to live this far uptown. Residents, however, soon arrived, seduced by its environs. Some of the more famous included the founder of New York University Medical School, Valentine Mott, and lawyer George Templeton Strong, Theodore Roosevelt, and Stanford White.

During the 1920s many buildings were torn down to give way to high-rise apartments. Others became private clubs that attracted the literati of the day. Several older structures remain and possess wonderful historic detail in their façade and iron work.

Previous page: Central Park.

Above: Bronze statue of Edwin Booth, brother of John Wilkes Booth, the man who assassinated President Abraham Lincoln in 1865.

These row houses speak to their eclectic historical pasts. According to some accounts, for instance, the Players' Club was the home of actor Edwin Booth, brother of John Wilkes Booth, the man who assassinated President Abraham Lincoln in 1865. A bronze statue of Edwin Booth, dressed as Shakespeare's Hamlet, stands inside the park.

Despite the massive real estate development in the neighborhood, the park and the square around it remain small and exclusive. This tony address houses some of the oldest luxury apartments in the city, and the large garden remains the only private park requiring a key.

This wonderful room in the Player's Club, once called the Reading Room, is known as the Sargent Room, in recognition of the three portraits by John Singer Sargent that hang here.

Battery Park and Lower Manhattan.

Battery Park City

Native Americans called the area around Battery Park and Battery Park City Capske Hook. With access to both the harbor and the Hudson River, Manhattan's southern tip was perfectly suited for fortification. Although they were never used for military purposes, Battery Park is named after the gun batteries that once jutted out of its shoreline.

Battery Park was ceded to the City of New York in 1823. Castle Clinton, the oldest building from the early days of Battery Park, was converted into a concert hall, and later the Emigrant Landing Depot, where it processed 7.7 million people. This operation was moved to the Barge Office in 1890 and then to Ellis Island in 1892.

At this point, Castle Clinton was converted yet again, this time to house an aquarium that entertained and delighted New Yorkers until 1941.

The park is also home to several memorials, including the East Coast Memorial in tribute to the 4,601 servicemen who lost their lives in the Atlantic Ocean during World War II. A bronze art deco–style eagle stands at the head of the monument, located near the end of Dewey Promenade. Separately, there is a temporary memorial for the victims of the World Trade Center collapse. *The Sphere* is a sculpture by Fritz Koenig with an eternal flame that was lit in September 2002.

To the north of Battery Park, landfill from the construction of the World Trade Center in the 1970s was used to fill the 300-foot stretch that separated Battery Park from the island of Manhattan. It is from this stretch of new man-made land that Battery Park City was designed, under the Battery Park City Authority (BPCA) and Wallace K. Harrison.

Battery Park City, following Harrison's plan to combine housing and social services, represents an urbane mix of public parks and private real estate. Construction was halted by a municipal fiscal crisis early on, but development later resumed. By the mid-1990s, the area boasted a marina and outdoor plaza, public art installations, a ferry to the Statue of Liberty and Ellis Island (tickets sold in the old Castle Clinton building), and charming waterside views.

Along with Castle Clinton, Battery Park's long maritime past can be found in a slow walk around the many monuments and memorials to soldiers, immigrants, workers, and explorers that dot the park.

East Coast World War II Memorial.

The Bronx Zoo

For years, the Bronx Zoo's jingle was "Something's always happening at the zoo." Although the slogan has changed, the promise of excitement remains at one of the world's foremost zoos.

Since its 1899 opening, the 265-acre zoo has delighted children of all ages with its astonishing variety of wildlife. More than 4,000 animals from 500 species are exhibited in the World of Reptiles, Butterfly Garden, Tiger Mountain, Sea Lion Pool, and Bird Valley, among other attractions.

Its most innovative exhibit, the Congo Gorilla Forest, welcomes visitors to a 6.5-acre site showing the inner workings of an African rain forest. More than 400 animals from 55 species make their home in this detailed recreation. Gorillas represent a highlight of the exhibit. A clever layout allows the curious to see the gorillas' behavior up close. Unlike King Kong, the most famous gorilla ever to arrive in New York, these gorillas eat, sleep, and mate in relative peace, just a few miles north of the Empire State Building.

The Congo Gorilla Forest exhibit is the latest in a serious of pioneering exhibits. The Bronx Zoo has traditionally led the wildlife conservation movement with its open plan, shunning animal cages in favor of naturalistic habitats.

The African Plains exhibit was the first zoo exhibit to put a predator and its prey in the same location. Lions are separated from nyala by moats, but visitors can see them simultaneously.

Girl viewing a Siberian tiger at the Bronx Zoo's Tiger Mountain, a year-round exhibit.

Right: American flamingo at the Bronx Zoo.

Below: Lowland gorilla at the Bronx Zoo's award-winning Congo Gorilla Forest, a 6.5-acre African rain forest habitat that is home to two troops of gorillas as well as okapi, red river hogs, mandrills, Wolf's monkeys, DeBrazza's monkeys, birds, fish, snakes, and other animals from this part of the world.

Although the glitter of Manhattan commands the lion's share of attention from New Yorkers and tourists, those who tear themselves away find that a trip to the Bronx Zoo is well worthwhile.

The Steinhardt Conservatory.

Brooklyn Botanic Garden

The site of the Brooklyn Botanic Garden began as part of the Brooklyn Institute of Arts and Sciences on a discarded tract of meadowlands previously used as an ash dump. In 1897, the New York State legislature reserved 39 acres for a botanic garden. The Brooklyn Botanic Garden now comprises 52 acres.

Like the other institutions that frame the cultural hub of this area, including the Brooklyn

Museum and Brooklyn Public Library, the garden is devoted to public education. For much of its history, the Brooklyn Botanic Garden distinguished itself from other gardens by promoting and expanding its educational role in the area, establishing one of the world's first children's gardens in 1914.

During its early years, the Brooklyn Botanic Garden acquired a number of collections that remain an enduring part of its appeal. The Rock Garden, bonsai collections, and fifty varieties of cherry blossom trees are among some of these longstanding exhibits.

The close of the twentieth century brought a number of restorations and additions to the garden. The Conservatory was added in 1988, for instance, showcasing an extensive indoor plant collection. The Japanese Hill-and-Pond garden was restored in 2000, drawing thousands of visitors every year. Exhibits such as the Hill-and-Pond Garden and the global plant habitats of the Conservatory are a hallmark of the Brooklyn Botanic Garden's lush, communal setting.

Cranford Rose Garden.

Bryant Park

Bryant Park is a charming and beautiful place to relax in the heart of the city, located at 42nd Street between 5th and 6th avenues. New Yorkers enjoy its many features which include a lush, grassy lawn, a carousel, a bar and restaurant, a kiosk selling discounted tickets for cultural events, free movie screenings in the summer, and an ice rink in the winter. It is a favorite spot with New York's stylish crowd due, in part, to its proximity to the Fashion District, and for several years it has hosted Fashion Week, a popular event featuring the work of international fashion designers. Thousands of paparazzi, celebrities, fashion editors, and couture clothing buyers complete for front-row seats at this extravaganza.

Although it has star status in the twenty-first century, Bryant Park sprang from humble beginnings in the nineteenth century, going through several metamorphoses before its current incarnation. In 1823, the land now known as Bryant Park was designated as a potter's field. At that time, this section of Manhattan was countryside well north of the Manhattan population. The cemetery was decommissioned in 1840 when it became apparent that urban sprawl would overtake the area.

In 1847, following the construction of one of the city's most imposing edifices, the Croton Distributing Reservoir, on the present site of the New York Public Library, the city designated the former potter's field to its west as a public park called Reservoir Square. During the Civil War, the Union Army held military drills in Reservoir Square. In 1853–54, New York's first "World's Fair," the Crystal Palace Exhibition, took place on the site of Bryant Park. The remarkable iron and glass structure erected to house the fair remained standing until 1858, when it burned down.

In 1884, the park took on its present name. William Cullen Bryant, its designee, achieved a reputation as a poet and newspaper editor as he campaigned for the creation of public parks in the city.

During the twentieth century, Bryant Park underwent a number of changes. New York Parks Commissioner Robert Moses turned his gaze towards its grounds during the Great Depression and changed the vista to include a large central lawn and an imposing set of stone balustrades. Although designed to make the grounds a welcome respite from the pressures of street life, the balustrades instead separated the park's interior from public traffic and discouraged wide usage.

By the 1970s, the park had become run-down and was considered a dangerous place at night. To rectify the problem, Bryant Park was renovated extensively. The park was reopened in 1992.

The Bryant Park rink is 17,000 square feet, about half the size of the Wollman Rink in Central Park and twice as big as the rink at Rockefeller Center.

Conservatory Garden, north end, Central Park. The six-acre Conservatory Garden is Central Park's only formal garden. It takes its name from the huge glass conservatory that once stood on this same spot, built in 1898. The present garden, which opened to the public in 1937, is, in fact, three gardens representing different landscape styles: Italian, French, and English.

Central Park

According to historians, Central Park is the first landscaped public park in the United States. It was the vision of wealthy benefactors who enjoyed the public grounds of Europe and thought that a major park in the city would raise New York's reputation. It was also the idea of visionaries who thought nature had the power to uplift. They hoped it would become a natural preserve in the middle of the city, a welcome alternative to the challenges of urban life. A contest to design Central Park was held in 1857. Frederick Law Olmsted and Calvert Vaux submitted what was called the "Greensward Plan" and won; their design featured green space that was largely unspoiled by structures.

A total of 843 acres, Central Park turned out to be a major public works project of the nineteenth century. The land for the park was chosen, in part, because its irregular terrain of swamps and bluffs, punctuated by rocky outcroppings, discouraged private real estate development. Although swamplands on an uneven grade may have prevented speculators from selling real estate, these conditions did not deter New York's poorer residents from settling there.

Some of these residents were hired by the local government to develop the park. Irish pig farmers and German gardeners were among the immigrants who planted trees and shrubs and spread gunpowder across the hills. Some say the amount of gunpowder used on Central Park was greater than the firepower used in the Civil War battle of Gettysburg. The park was completed quickly in 1859, but construction displaced approximately 1,600 poor immigrants who had brought the project to fruition.

Central Park was initially used only by wealthy New Yorkers who lived nearby. Eventually the park enjoyed a wider constituency, many of whom changed its spirit and use according to their needs and desires. Recreation facilities were created, and eventually the reservoir was drained to become the Great Lawn. During the 1930s, federal funds were obtained to build other fields. Today its thousands of trees attract 215 different species of birds, making Central Park an unlikely bird sanctuary in the city's core.

*No single other activity can match a carriage ride through
Central Park.*

Gapstow Bridge arches over the northeast end of the pond. This is the second bridge of the same name on this site. The original, whose design is attributed to Jacob Wrey Mould, was built in 1874.

During the 1950s and early 1960s, Central Park increasingly sponsored public festivals—featuring the works of Shakespeare and artistry of the New York Philharmonic. By the late 1960s, Mayor John Lindsay had begun to promote rock concerts and the park became an outlet for artistic expression. Runners, cyclists, and other athletes are drawn to the 6.2-mile circular road that winds through the park, closed to cars except during weekday rush hours. Children wait with great excitement to ride the carousel and to visit the zoo in winter.

Upkeep of the park is maintained by the Central Park Conservancy. Although maintenance and safety declined with New York's fortunes in the 1970s, millions of dollars have been spent for the refurbishment of the park in the last 20 years. As a result, the park has rebounded as an attraction for tourists, hipsters, students, rollerbladers, people-watchers, and anyone looking for a free place to relax.

The southeast corner of Central Park was from its inception, and remains today, the most heavily used Park entrance.

Grand Army Plaza

Originally called Prospect Park Plaza, Brooklyn's Grand Army Plaza represents a wonderful assortment of monuments at the foot of Prospect Park in the Park Slope neighborhood of Brooklyn. Grand Army Plaza was built by Frederick Law Olmsted and Calvert Vaux, the designers of Prospect Park and Central Park.

As the main entrance to its grounds, Olmsted and Vaux wanted the plaza to distinguish itself from the park's rustic interior. The soaring arch, designed later by John H. Duncan, introduced European grandeur to the area. Duncan, who also built Grant's Tomb in Riverside Park, may have added more majesty than either Olmsted or Vaux had originally desired.

The plaza was later renamed Grand Army Plaza in honor of the Union army. General William Tecumseh Sherman is said to have laid

Memorial Arch.

The Bailey Fountain.

the first stone. Four horse chariots, also military symbols, were added to the arch by Frederick MacMonnies in 1898.

A memorial of a far different sort, the Bailey Fountain, sits back away from the park near Flatbush Avenue. Built in 1932 by architect Edgerton Swarthout and sculptor Eugene Savage, it represents philanthropist Frank Bailey's personal memorial to his wife and features an intricate set of water spouts dancing among a group of mythical figures.

According to the Prospect Park Alliance, Grand Army Plaza is also the site of the second-largest open-air Greenmarket in New York City. Every Saturday, shoppers enjoy more than 600 varieties of farm-fresh fruits, vegetables, baked goods, dairy products, and more. Close to the Brooklyn Botanic Garden, the Brooklyn Museum and Brooklyn Library, Grand Army Plaza is an integral part of the public culture in the great borough of Brooklyn.

Prospect Park holds many attractions, including an ice skating rink, a lake and boat-house, a band shell for outdoor concerts, a zoo, nature trails, a baseball diamond, bike path, Audubon Center, and playgrounds.

General Grant National Memorial

General Ulysses S. Grant, eighteenth president of the United States, settled in New York after his presidency. He died here in 1885, having spent the last five years of his life in the city. As the victorious commanding general of the Union army, Grant is credited as the defender of the Union. He was respected by both the North and South, and was a very popular American when he died, both domestically and internationally. Designed by John H. Duncan, the General Grant National Memorial—or Grant's Tomb—was completed in 1897, and is the largest tomb in America. The president lies in a twin sarcophagus alongside his wife, Julia. He is the only U.S. President to have a final resting place in New York City.

The tomb blends well with the landscape of Riverside Park. The park's four-mile path moves in concert with the rocky terrain and valley below, and provides high views of both the Hudson River and the city. An ideal place for commemoration, the park is home to other monuments as well. Anna Hyatt's Joan of Arc is located at 93rd Street and Riverside Drive. A statue of Eleanor Roosevelt, sculpted by Penelope Jencks, sits on 72nd Street.

Grant's Tomb is operated by the National Park Service, a branch of the U.S. Department of the Interior. The tomb is distinguished from the other monuments in the park by its majestic style, long history, detailed mosaics, and sheer size. For many years, the tomb was a major attraction for visitors. Though it fell into disrepair during the late twentieth century, renovation has restored it to some of its original grandeur.

View of Manhattan from Green-Wood Cemetery.

Detail of gatehouse designed in Gothic Revival style.

Green-Wood Cemetery

Green-Wood Cemetery is located at one of Brooklyn's highest summits. Founded in 1838 as the third rural cemetery in America, it was a leading tourist attraction by the 1850s, attracting 500,000 visitors per year. By the 1860s, the *New York Times* was reporting that "It is the ambition of the New Yorker to live upon the Fifth Avenue, to take his airings in the [Central] Park, and to sleep with his fathers in GreenWood [*sic*]." Inspired by Mount Auburn cemetery in Cambridge Massachusetts, the cemetery was surveyed and designed by civil engineer David Bates Douglass. He and his financial backers thought that the area's views (and proximity to Manhattan) made the location ideal.

In keeping with the dramatic landscape, a number of interesting architectural features mark the cemetery, such as the gatehouse on 5th Avenue and 25th Street, designed in Gothic Revival style by Richard Upjohn. A number of famous New Yorkers are buried in this nonsectarian cemetery, among them abolitionist Henry Ward Beecher, Louis Comfort Tiffany, Horace Greeley, Lola Montez, Charles Ebbets, politicians Henry George and William "Boss" Tweed, piano makers Henry and William Steinway, inventors Peter Cooper and Samuel F.B. Morse, activist Margaret Sanger, composer Leonard Bernstein, and crime figure Joey Gallo.

There are also monuments that mark historic events in New York's past, including one that commemorates the victims of the Brooklyn Theatre fire in 1876 as well as another that marks the graves of those who died in the *General Slocum* steamship disaster of 1904.

Washington Square Park

Washington Square Park is located near an old Nativ American settlement, where the Sappokanican Indians lived off marshland fed by Minetta Brook. Later, Washington Square Park served as the city's first known potter's field or cemetery. (In 1869, the city chose Hart Island, a small land mass in Long Island Sound, as its major potter's field.) In subsequent years, the area around Washington Square Park served as a place for public hangings and then, a parade ground.

In 1827, the city acquired the area for use as park land. The park was largely empty for several years, but it was redesigned and refurbished after the establishment of the New York Parks Department in 1870. During this period, the city erected monuments to soldier Giuseppe Garibaldi and engineer Alexander Lyman Holley in the grounds, and also built a temporary arch commemorating the inauguration of George Washington. The provisional structure was replaced by a permanent one designed by Stanford White in 1895. It remains a signature feature of the park.

Washington Square Park North is home to a row of architecturally significant houses built in the nineteenth century. Novelist Henry James set his famous novel *Washington Square* on that street. The landmark structures include a Greek Revival group of houses from numbers 19 to 26.

Fifth Avenue traffic ran through the park for many years. Buses used the space around the fountain as a turnaround, and their engines idled between runs. The park's air quality improved after the street was closed off in the 1960s. Free of traffic and in close vicinity to New York University and the entertainment venues of Greenwich Village, Washington Square Park became a natural site for public congregation. It drew all kinds of visitors to its fountain, grassy picnic areas, and chess tables. Beatniks, folk artists, political protesters, students, and tourists all gathered and reveled in its open spaces. The area around the fountain remains popular for people-watching, hanging out with friends, and impromptu street performances.

Landmarks: Temples of Worship, Commerce, and Sport

Abyssinian Baptist Church

The Abyssinian Baptist Church is one of the oldest Protestant congregations in the United States. The congregation was founded by free blacks who refused to adhere to the segregated seating practices of the First Baptist Church of New York in Lower Manhattan. According to historians, these dissenters withdrew from the Church and allied with a handful of Ethiopian merchants in the city to create their own congregational vision.

Throughout the nineteenth and early twentieth centuries, the Church moved uptown to a few locations. The congregation eventually found a permanent home due to the vision of (then) pastor Adam Clayton Powell Sr., who purchased lots on 138th Street between Lenox and 7th Avenues in 1908. Completed in 1923, the building's impressive architecture is matched only by its remarkable history. The 1920s were an exciting time in Harlem; the Harlem Renaissance was at its height. Moreover, just a few blocks away, firebrands like radical Marcus Garvey inspired masses with early visions of black pride and nationalism. Adam Clayton Powell Sr.'s Baptist services may have struck a more tempered note than Garvey had, but his message reverberated with the expectant tenor of the time.

In the late 1930s, Powell stepped down from his post and passed the position to his son, Adam Clayton Powell Jr. In his myriad of roles, Adam Clayton Powell Jr. was a politically engaged and brash figure, attuned to the struggles of the Harlem community. He tapped into the liberation messages that Christianity shared with social justice movements and drew his support form a variety of quarters—including Christians, communists, and black nationalists.

Successors to Adam Clayton Powell Jr. in this post include the Rev. Samuel DeWitt Proctor and the Rev. Calvin O. Butts III. Abyssinian Baptist Church has served as host to compelling figures over the years, like Leontyne Price and Kathleen Battle, both of whom drew on its rich history and heady acoustic surroundings to sing the great yearnings of the black freedom struggle.

Previous page: View of Manhattan, George Washington Bridge, and New Jersey.

The Hotel Chelsea

The Hotel Chelsea was converted from co-op apartments to a hotel in 1905. From the start, its artsy clientele distinguished it from other notable hotels in Manhattan. Early visitors included Sarah Bernhardt, O. Henry, Lillian Russell, and Mark Twain.

During the post-World War II period and well into the Sixties, the Chelsea continued to draw celebrities to its doors. Dylan Thomas, Arthur Miller, and Bob Dylan all stayed in its elegantly simple rooms. In addition to being a place to see and be seen, the Chelsea shepherded a number of artists and their works to completion. During their tenure there several created some of their most celebrated works. Various authors took up

residence at the Chelsea as they completed their seminal works. These include Thomas Wolfe of *You Can't Go Home Again*; William Burroughs of *Naked Lunch*, and Arthur C. Clarke of *2001*. The eclectic mix of authors stands credit to the hotel's diverse imaginative lore. The Chelsea even wove itself directly into the artistry of Andy Warhol's film *The Chelsea Girls* (1966) and Leonard Cohen's song *Chelsea Hotel No. 2*.

A landmark building, the Hotel Chelsea is an engaging structure to behold. It is true to its past, and artwork from around the world decorates its walls. Its Victorian-style and ornately detailed iron balconies still charm the eye and inspire the mind.

The Peace Fountain depicts the struggle of good and evil. The forces of good, represented by the figure of the archangel Michael, triumph by decapitating Satan. The fountain is encircled by figures cast in bronze from pieces sculpted by children.

The Cathedral of St. John the Divine

The Cathedral of St. John the Divine belongs to the Episcopal Diocese of New York and is the seat of its bishop. It is located at Amsterdam Avenue and West 112th Street.

From the beginning, builders encountered complications in its construction. Just reaching bedrock to build the foundation took over two years of digging and required the substantial financial backing of J.P. Morgan to achieve. Meanwhile, the architectural firm of Heins and LaFarge was also preoccupied with Diocesan House (completed 1909) and the Chapel of St. Columba (completed 1911), slowing construction of the cathedral even further. Finally, shortly after the consecration of the Great Choir and Crossing in April 1911, a new architect was chosen to complete construction of the cathedral.

The new designer, Ralph Adams Cram, preferred the French Gothic style. He worked with the existing Byzantine-Romanesque structure to marry the two, and features of the earlier design remain evident in the apse, choir, and crossing of the church.

Along with these hybridized niches, the Cathedral of St. John the Divine features a number of interesting details. Rumor has it that the cathedral's bronze doors were cast by Barbedienne, the same man who cast the Statue of Liberty. The cathedral is still under construction, and community and church members trained in masonry do much of the labor on the church. Overall, its stained-glass windows are a playful mix of biblical and modern images. Its large size remains its outstanding feature.

The Chrysler Building

Automobile executive Walter P. Chrysler brought the Chrysler Building to fruition when he took over the lease in mid-construction. As it is, the building stands as a fitting tribute to the modern age, a powerful legacy of the mechanic-turned-millionaire. His bold brilliance, along with the energy of Brooklyn-born architect William Van Alen, created one of New York's most beloved buildings in 1930. The building was the tallest in the world until it was surpassed by the Empire State Building one year later. Although Chrysler did not make dramatic changes to Van Alen's original design, some historians believe that the building's signature features are the result of his input.

Many of these details sit high up. Whether steel gargoyles, giant radiator caps, or the eagle heads that grace the corners of the 61st floor, each demands singular attention. The building's helmet top is perhaps its most unique feature, playing on an automobile steel cladding theme. Inside, *Transportation and Human Endeavor*, a mural of the heroic worker painted by Edward Trumbull, idealizes the American dream of perseverance and ingenuity against a backdrop of the engine of industry. A major 1999 restoration uncovered fascinating ceiling murals.

The building was declared a landmark in 1978, and it is now owned by Tishman Speyer Properties.

Aerial view of the Chrysler Building.

The Dakota

The Dakota is said to have been named because at the time it was built, the Upper West Side of Manhattan was sparsely inhabited and considered as remote as the Dakota Territory. Although some critics thought it foolish to build in a remote part of New York City, investor Edward Clark saw the gamble differently. He banked on the idea that clientele would appreciate the advantages of living away from the harried urban core. The Dakota was built between 1882 and 1884 and was fully rented by the time of its completion.

High above the 72nd Street entrance, the figure of a Dakota Indian keeps watch. The Dakota is built around a central courtyard, accessible through the arched passage of the main

entrance, an opening large enough that horse-drawn carriages could pass through, letting their passengers disembark sheltered from the weather, then exit on 73rd Street. The building's high gables and deep roofs with a profusion of dormers, terracotta spandrels and panels, niches, balconies, and balustrades give it a North German Renaissance character, an echo of a Hanseatic town hall.

The Dakota's success prompted the construction of many other luxury apartment buildings in New York City. Over the years, the Dakota has served as an exclusive residence for many celebrities. In December 1980, singer John Lennon was killed in front of the building, marking its glorious past with a touch of sadness.

The Empire State Building

The Empire State Building, located on 5th Avenue between 33rd and 34th streets, soars to 1,250 feet (381 meters) in the city skyline. Designed by architects Shreve, Lamb, and Harmon, it was completed in 1931 and superseded the Chrysler Building as the tallest building in New York, holding onto the title until the completion of the World Trade Center in the 1970s.

Although it took nearly twenty years to bring the idea to practical fruition, the Empire State Building took less than two years to build. Workers were subjected to assembly-line efficiency at the behest of its investors: former officer in the General Motors Company John J. Raskob, industrialist Pierre S. du Pont, and former New York governor Alfred E. Smith.

At the peak of construction, a work force of nearly 3,500 was assembled. Photographer Lewis Hine was commissioned to document the construction of the building. His pictures capture both the ordinary and extraordinary working lives of his subjects. Among some of these workers were Mohawk Indians known for their ability to work high steel. These ironworkers helped build a number of city structures including the George Washington Bridge and the World Trade Center.

Like many of the tall buildings in New York, the Empire State Building represented a feat of

engineering. When it was completed, Alfred E. Smith championed, much as Chrysler had before him, the "brains, brawn, ingenuity, and the muscle of mankind." This was partially a credit to himself and his industry, but also a plain appreciation of those workers who invested their labor in its construction.

The building gained early notoriety in the movie *King Kong*. Despite its fame, leasing it was slow, and its detractors dubbed it the "Empty State" Building.

Tenants eventually filled the structure, and it thrives as a popular tourist attraction. The Empire State Building regained the title of tallest building in New York after the destruction of the World Trade Center in 2001.

The Flatiron Building

Chicago architect Daniel H. Burnham built the Flatiron Building, located on 5th Avenue and Broadway at 23rd Street, to draw business to the area in 1902. The building became an extraordinarily successful part of the commercial district.

Scholars suggest that the Flatiron Building speaks to architectural trends introduced at the 1893 World's Columbian Exposition in Chicago and stands as a lesser-known icon of the skyscraper era. Indeed, beneath the traditional Italian Renaissance limestone and terra-cotta shell rests a steel frame that secures its twenty stories against the city winds.

Its façade and steely poise have nothing on its unique shape. Although its triangular figure simply conforms to the fate of its plot,

the building drew admirers for its original design. Contemporaries thought the building resembled a flatiron or a ship, and pedestrians standing near its base compared the winds that wrapped around its six-foot apex to gusts on a shoreline.

Beloved by many New Yorkers, the Flatiron Building has animated and inspired locals and visitors since its creation. Photographed by Edward Steichen, Alfred Stieglitz, and Berenice Abbott, it is also featured in the paintings of John Sloan and the writings of O. Henry. According to some, when film actress Katherine Hepburn was asked to compare herself to a building, Hepburn immediately rejoined: "The Flatiron Building." Her answer suggests something of the iconoclasm of its appealing Janus face.

The Hotel Theresa

The Hotel Theresa, designed by George and Edward Blum, is located on 7th Avenue and 125th Street. It opened in 1913 and its thirteen stories were once the tallest in Harlem. Like the landmark Apollo Theater before it, the hotel did not admit blacks at first. It was desegregated in 1940. The change occurred after Love B. Woods, a black businessman, bought the hotel in 1937, and it became known as the Waldorf of Harlem.

That same year, renowned prize fighter Joe Louis celebrated his new world heavyweight title against James T. Braddock in the hotel's elegant interior.

Ensconced in a lively area near the Savoy Ballroom and Apollo Theater, the Hotel Theresa has been patronized by many celebrated figures in black history. These include Josephine Baker and Muhammad Ali. In 1960, Cuban president Fidel Castro was evicted from the Shelburne Hotel. In response to the expulsion, Castro moved his entourage to the Theresa. There he received Soviet leader Nikita Khrushchev, and Egypt's president Gamal Abdel Nasser. The hotel was also the headquarters of many community and national organizations such as the March on Washington led by A. Philip Randolph, and Malcolm X's Organization of Afro-American Unity, underscoring the fact that Harlem was a critical center of the black world.

Unfortunately, the hotel closed in 1970 and the building was converted to office space.

The Plaza Hotel

The Plaza Hotel is situated on the corner of 5th Avenue and Central Park South. It was designed by architect Henry J. Hardenbergh and opened to the public in October 1907.

Hardenbergh designed the Plaza Hotel in the style of French Renaissance Chateaux, creating an image that declares to the world outside the opulence and classic elegance of the atmosphere inside, down to the very last detail. This style could have been influenced by the mansion of Cornelius Vanderbilt II, which used to be between 58th and 59th streets, to the south of the Plaza. It too was built in the French Renaissance Chateau style, and was designed by George Browne Post. In its time, it was the grandest of the Fifth Avenue mansions of the Gilded Age.

Over the years, the Plaza has hosted the Duchess and Duke of Windsor, Frank Lloyd Wright, the Beatles, and many other ambassadors, dignitaries, and Hollywood stars. The hotel has been featured in dozens of movies, plays, and TV shows, including *The Way We Were, Annie,* and *North by Northwest.*

The Plaza Hotel was made into a historical landmark in 1969. It was bought in 2004 by developer Elad Properties for $675 million; the hotel was closed in 2005 for major interior renovations. It is scheduled to reopen in 2007 with luxury hotel rooms, residential condominiums, and retail space.

Riverside Church

Riverside Church began as the Fifth Avenue Baptist Church on 5th Avenue at 46th Street in 1860. It has since become an interdenominational church, renowned for its interracial and international congregation, on the Upper West Side of Manhattan. John D. Rockefeller Jr. donated millions to create an inclusive church for all Christians. In keeping with this mission, he installed the pacifist preacher Harry Emerson Fosdick in 1924 to serve as its first minister.

The new building was designed by Harry C. Pelton and Charles Collens. Completed in 1930, Riverside Church lies along Riverside Drive between 120th and 122nd streets, one of the highest points in Manhattan.

The church includes fascinating architectural details such as intricate stone carvings, original Renaissance windows, and stained glass. It also has a labyrinth on the floor adapted from the maze in France's Chartres Cathedral. The Gothic structure houses the Laura Spelman Rockefeller Memorial Carillon, a gift of John D. Rockefeller Jr. in memory of his mother.

A number of people have given important speeches from its pulpit. The Reverend Dr. Martin Luther King Jr. delivered a sermon here. South African President Nelson Mandela spoke at a celebration in his honor. U.N. Secretary General Kofi Annan consoled New Yorkers after the tragedy of September 11, 2001.

Since 1989, Dr. James A. Forbes Jr. has served as Senior Minister. His outreach to the community has included racial justice initiatives, emancipation from poverty, health and wellness, and other healing issues.

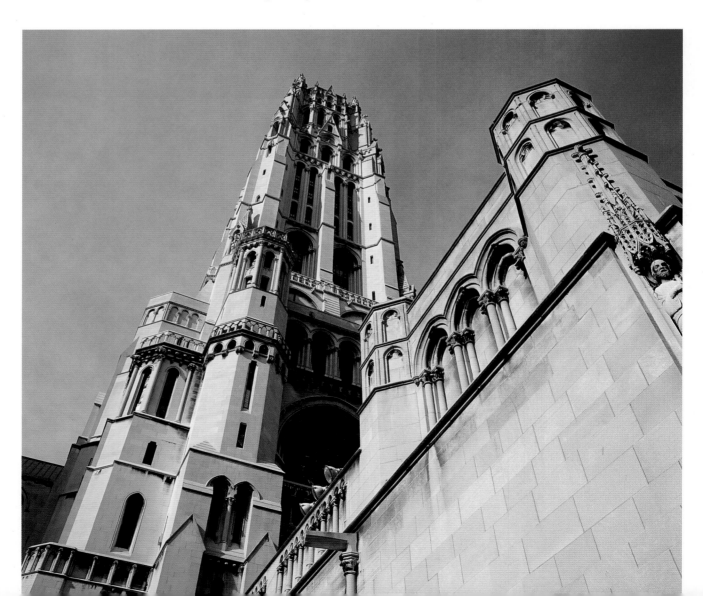

Arthur Ashe Stadium

The U.S. Open at Arthur Ashe Stadium in the Billie Jean King National Tennis Center remains an extraordinarily popular spot for locals and globetrotters alike. With its hard courts and fast play, its bustling crowds and air traffic, the stadium captures a slice of the city's vibrancy and its grounds remain home to one of New York's venerable sporting traditions.

The Open's modern incarnation began in New York in 1968 in Forest Hills, moving to Flushing in 1978. Some of the most famous players in the world took home titles on this urban landscape. In 1997, the championship match moved next door to the newly built Arthur Ashe Stadium, named for the championship player and humanitarian who died in 1993.

Arthur Ashe Stadium looms significantly larger than its predecessors, seating over 22,500 fans. Some say the Arthur Ashe Stadium has revitalized the U.S. Open, attracting a new generation of audiences. Others feel slightly outsized by its grandeur, missing the intimacy of earlier incarnations.

St. Patrick's Cathedral

St. Patrick's Cathedral, located on 5th Avenue and 50th Street, is the seat of the Roman Catholic Archdiocese of New York and its archbishop, Edward Cardinal Egan. Each year over 3 million people visit St. Patrick's Cathedral, which seats 2,200.

The cathedral, designed by James Renwick Jr., was begun in 1858 by Archbishop John Hughes to replace the original St. Patrick's Cathedral, which is used today as a parish church in New York. The cornerstone was laid in August of that year, and, after a suspension of work during the years of The Civil War, John Cardinal McCloskey, the first American cardinal, resumed work in 1865, opening the doors in May 1879. The archbishops of New York are buried in a crypt under the high altar. Their honorary hats, called galeros, hang from the ceiling over their tombs.

James Renwick was the architect for the cathedral in the 1850s, although the Lady Chapel was designed later by Charles Mathews in 1906. According to scholars, its traditional Gothic Revival style exhibits a decidedly French influence. The St. Michael and St. Louis altar was

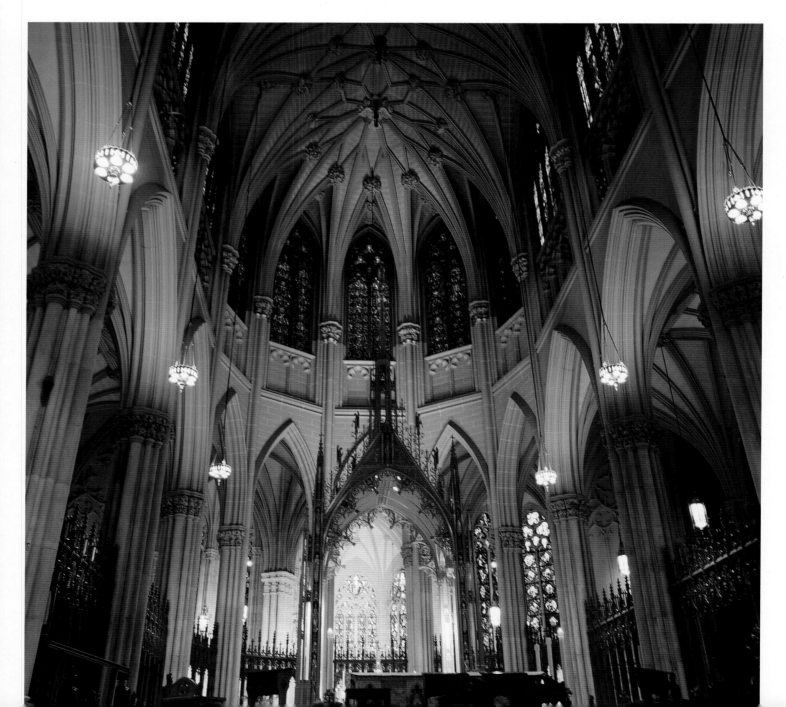

designed by Tiffany and Company. The St. Elizabeth altar was designed by Paolo Medici of Rome. The exterior length of the cathedral is about 405 feet (123 meters); the width is 274 feet (83.5 meters). The spires rise 330 feet (100.5 meters) from street level. The Pieta is three times larger than the Pieta in St. Peter's, Rome.

From its inception, the church served many of New York's poorer Catholic immigrants. Over the years, a number of Catholic luminaries including Popes Paul VI and John Paul II have visited the cathedral. It is also known as the site for the wakes for former Governor Alfred E. Smith and U.S. Attorney General Robert F. Kennedy.

Trinity Church

An Anglican church, Trinity Church derived from a royal charter under William III. As the third church to stand on this site, the building dates back to 1846. Its Gothic Revival style was designed by Robert Upjohn, founder of the American Institute of Architects. Columbia University formed, in part, from its parish. The Trinity School, one of the oldest continuously operating schools in Manhattan, was born of its early charity school.

Chapels were added to the church over time. The most famous is St. Paul's Chapel, built by Andrew Gautier. Some argue that St. Paul's is the oldest public building in continuous use in Manhattan. It is said that George Washington worshiped there during the two years that New York City was the capital of the nation. More recently, St. Paul's Chapel served as a central site in the relief effort following the World Trade Center's collapse in September 2001.

A testament to its history—a number of New Yorkers are buried in the churchyard, including Robert Fulton, the first person to successfully apply steam power to ship locomotion; Alexander Hamilton, the first secretary of the treasury; and Albert Gallitin, founding trustee of New York University.

Lore has it that, before Times Square, New Yorkers would gather around Trinity Church to ring in the New Year, as its Gothic spire has long been part of Lower Manhattan's skyline. Even though it is now dwarfed by its steely neighbors, its constancy in the face of historic change gives Trinity Church a unique command of city space.

The United Nations

The tract of land where the United Nations sits used to be sandwiched between Dutch Hill and Turtle Bay. Rumor has it that Dutch Hill used to be inhabited by criminal gangs and wild herds of goat. Turtle Bay lore fairs somewhat better by comparison. Some say poet Edgar Allen Poe boated to the bay, originally a natural shelter from the elements, to enjoy its bucolic reprieve.

Now a staple of the riverfront, the U.N.'s place in New York was not sure from its founding. The city competed with other locations for the site of its headquarters, but New York won the commission.

The United Nations Headquarters was designed by an international team of more than ten architects headed by Wallace K. Harrison. Work on the complex began in 1947 and was completed in 1952. The Secretariat Building reaches 39 stories high with places for 155 global member states, a number that shifts with geopolitical time.

Across from the United Nations, in the middle of the East River, lies a small island (formed by excavated subway tunnel work) that is popularly called U Thant, designated in memory of the U.N. secretary general of the same name. Redecorated with trees and flowers, it is a small bird sanctuary.

The U.N. may not be an island of its own, but it possesses its own police force, fire department, and postal service. The City of New York agreed to give the United Nations waterfront and street rights at its inception. The grounds of the organization are not part of the United States, or bound to the laws of any nation, state, or city.

The Woolworth Building

Located on Broadway between Park Place and Barclay Street, completed in 1913, the Woolworth Building once held the title of tallest building in the world. Frank Woolworth, dime-store chain owner, commissioned the building in collaboration with the Irving National Bank. Rumor has it that Woolworth paid for it in cash.

The Woolworth Building was designed by Cass Gilbert, an apprentice of McKim, Mead, and White, and engineered by Gunvald Aus. Its Gothic style is plainly evident in its terra-cotta exterior. According to scholars, it was one of the first buildings to combine a Gothic aesthetic with a skyscraper's height. Indeed, the striking interior distracts most onlookers from the steel frame that bears its weight to withstand high winds.

It was dubbed a "cathedral of commerce" at its dedication due to its lavish lobby, which is endowed with stained-glass windows, gold leaf murals, and vaulted ceilings. Its commercial nature was equally central to its design. Work by Tom Johnson in the lobby features many figures involved in its construction. Engineer Gunvald Aus is depicted as one of the gargoyles in the lobby's halls. Another gargoyle shows Woolworth himself, assiduously counting dimes. A model for skyscrapers after the war, the Woolworth Building remains a compelling structure to explore, inside and out.

An overview of Yankee Stadium during a major-league baseball game between the New York Yankees and the Detroit Tigers.

Yankee Stadium

For many fans, Yankee Stadium is one of baseball's cathedrals, sacred ground. Fans revere its history, and what a history it has been. The "house that Babe Ruth built" is home to one the most successful sports franchises in the U.S.

If Yankee Stadium was built to accommodate the crowds drawn to Babe Ruth's relentless hitting, the great slugger gladly obliged. Ruth's dramatic play broke records and continued to draw thousands. He was one of many famous Yankees. Younger fans might remember stars of the Steinbrenner era including Roger Clemens, Catfish Hunter, Reggie Jackson, Derek Jeter, Mariano Rivera, Bernie Williams, and others. Other Yankee legends include Yogi Berra, Joe DiMaggio, Whitey Ford, Lou Gehrig, Mickey Mantle, Roger Maris, and Don Mattingly.

A development plan to build a new Yankee Stadium has called the future of this building into question. Meanwhile, the team's search for a new home divides locals and sports fans alike. It may not be the oldest ballpark in the nation, but it is over 80 years old, nearly ancient by modern stadium standards. Some consider the idea of tearing down Yankee Stadium akin to the demolition the old Pennsylvania Station. However, a new stadium is expected to open in 2009.

Shea Stadium

The New York Mets are well known for having a loyal fan base. Despite the team's frequent five hundred record, faithful fans remain. Each year they sport expectant signs, from "Mets Magic" to the more contemporary mantra "You Gotta Believe," with fervor matched by few. The team has often risen to meet the hopes of its fans. The "Amazins" have won the World Series twice, in 1969 and 1986. Several players rose to fame in the franchise including Gary Carter, John Franco, Dwight Gooden, Keith Hernandez, Willie Mays, Mike Piazza, Tom Seaver, Darryl Strawberry, Rusty Staub, and Mookie Wilson.

The stadium's environment has some unique features. Planes jet against the breeze of the waterways around La Guardia to fly low and level over the large ballpark. Their presence captures the whistle and woof of city life. Fans cheer to the large red apple that rises in the air following a home run. This bulky three-dimensional mass, dated to some, stands as a welcome respite to the high-tech visuals that mark many modern ballparks.

In 2005, the town began to talk about a Mets plan to build a new stadium next door in the parking lot at Shea. Despite the real possibility of changing venues and tearing down the old stadium, the team's spirit is well established in the city. A telling symbol of the New York Mets is the circular insignia skyline of its logo. In recent history, Shea Stadium served as a relief center for city residents after the terrorist strike of September 11, 2001.

Mets playing at Shea Stadium.

Cultural Capital of the United States: Broadway, Museums, and Universities

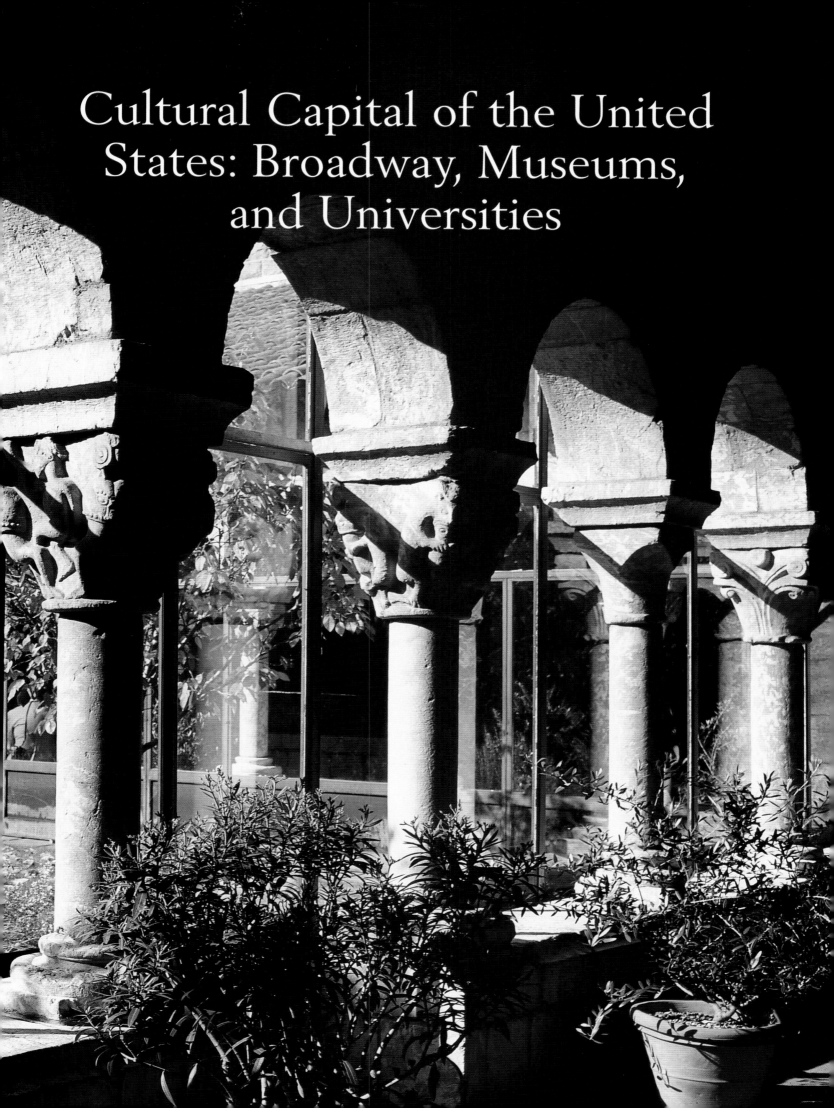

Broadway

From its early history, Broadway served as a major thoroughfare, a critical north/south route used by indigenous people and early settlers. The street still stretches the length of the island and touches on many parts of the city on its way. As a result, the 12-mile road has many moods and characters, unique to the individual neighborhoods that it passes through. Broadway is as much a part of Union Square as it is Times Square; it marks the east side of New York University as much as it does Columbia's campus on the west.

Although it winds its way from the top to the bottom of Manhattan, it is known world over for its midtown stretch, near Times Square. Like Wall Street, Broadway began as a street, but the name has become an international symbol. For theater lovers, Broadway represents the pinnacle of achievement.

Among the intensity and bustle of Times Square, one may be hard pressed to recall the street's long span. However, Broadway's vitality rests not in one place, but in the many communities and cultures it bridges along the way.

Below and opposite: Broadway theater district glitters at night.

Previous page: The Cloisters.

The Apollo Theater

Originally called Hurtig and Seamon's New (Burlesque) Theater, the Apollo opened its doors in 1914 to white audiences only.

The Hurtig and Seamon Theater was renamed the Apollo in 1925. The establishment began admitting African-American patrons in 1934, and subsequently featured performances by black artists such as Bessie Smith, Ethel Waters, Ella Fitzgerald, and Sarah Vaughan. It became the premier showplace for black entertainers.

To be sure, the Apollo was just one of a series of important cultural centers in a vibrant uptown scene. Here jazz, blues, and boogie-woogie seeped in and out of the theater's walls and could be heard in the Apollo as easily as it could in the lounges, dance halls, and cafes that dotted Harlem. By the 1960s, the Apollo had become a venue where performers like Duke Ellington, Diana Ross, Marvin Gaye, Michael Jackson, and others showcased their talents. As well as being a place of entertainment, the Apollo has long been an integral part of the Harlem community. In a mix of culture and politics that has long been a part of the African-American experience, actors such as Sidney Poitier, Ossie Davis, and Canada Lee have spoken on behalf of racial justice on its stage.

Converted into a movie theater in 1975, the Apollo obtained federal, state, and city landmark status less than a decade later, and enjoyed a renaissance in the 1980s. Featured live performances at the Apollo continue to entertain and inspire audiences. The theater's tradition of hosting major cultural and political events has extended into the twenty-first century.

Overlooking audience in the Apollo Theater.

The Audubon Theater and Ballroom

Thomas W. Lamb built the Audubon Theater and Ballroom in 1912 for William Fox, famed movie mogul and owner of 20th Century Fox Studios. In its early incarnation, the Audubon Theater and Ballroom served as performance venue for the likes of Fanny Brice. The theater was the first in the Washington Heights community to feature movies with sound, showing *The Jazz Singer* with Al Jolson.

On February 21, 1965, the Audubon etched its place in historical memory as the site where Malcolm X, a prominent voice in the black freedom movement and leader of the Organization of Afro-American Unity, was assassinated during a rally in the second-floor ballroom.

Despite its long and varied history, the building was slated for demolition, only to be pulled back from the brink of destruction by concerned citizens and historians. Columbia Presbyterian Medical Center purchased the building in the mid-1990s. Grassroots efforts by Harlem residents and other preservationists to designate the building as a landmark site of historical significance failed. Columbia Presbyterian built a new structure behind the old one, preserving the ornate terra-cotta façade of the original theater, an impressive reminder of the building's past. The university hospital also designated a portion of the renovated structure to the memory of Malcolm X.

Currently part of Columbia University's Audubon Biomedical Science and Technology Park, the building has been chosen as the future home of the Malcolm X Memorial Museum. The education and research center houses a memorial to the leader which consists, in part, of a mural painted by Daniel Galves and a life-sized statue of Malcolm X in the lobby.

Carnegie Hall

Designed in a neo-Renaissance style by architect and musician William B. Tuthill in 1891, Carnegie Hall was built on 57th Street at the corner of 7th Avenue, a location considered far uptown at the time. Its northern reach did not stop devotees of music from attending. Lore has it that the Whitneys, Fricks, Rockefellers, and Sloans were among those in attendance on opening night enjoying the work of Russian composer Pytor Ilyich Tchaikovsky.

Originally the hall consisted of four public spaces, or auditoriums. During its first century, 50,000 events took place in Carnegie Hall and 1,300 compositions made their world or American premiere on its stage.

A Carnegie Hall appearance became synonymous with success. Many performed their own works there, including Gustav Mahler, Aaron Copland, Igor Stravinsky, John Cage, and Philip Glass.

Largely known as a venue for classical pieces, Carnegie Hall has also featured major names in pop, folk, jazz, and rock and roll. The Beatles, Miles Davis, Ella Fitzgerald, Judy Garland, Benny Goodman, Woody Guthrie, Nina Simone, and Paul Robeson are known to have graced its stage. Carnegie Hall has left its mark on political history as well, hosting lectures by the likes of Winston Churchill and Theodore Roosevelt.

Threatened by demolition, the building was designated a national landmark in 1964, preserved from the wrecking ball by a devoted committee headed by violinist Isaac Stern. Many benefactors were involved in its later renovations. Upgraded and restored, the largest hall at Carnegie Hall has been dedicated to the memory of Isaac Stern.

The City College of New York

The City College of New York was founded by Townshend Harris and chartered by the New York State Legislature in 1847. Originally called the Free Academy, its aim was to provide poorer New Yorkers with a strong education. It stands as the oldest of the city universities in New York and served as the model for later City University of New York schools to follow.

During its early history, the institution provided an education to those who could not get a comparable one in the largely Protestant universities that served the national elite. As a result, City College attracted German and Russian Jews who had recently immigrated to the United States. By the 1930s, nearly four-fifths of the enrollees were Jewish.

Many of the structures that comprised City College were built from schist that had been excavated from subway tunnel work throughout the city. A striking amphitheater, paid for by Adolph Lewisohn, was torn down in 1973 and became a plaza.

Called by some "the poor man's Harvard," City College has long distinguished itself for its academic excellence. The college's exploding enrollment sparked the opening of Brooklyn and Queens campuses. They later transformed into Brooklyn College and Queens College, respectively.

From the 1930s through the 1950s, City College took on a decidedly progressive bent, and was well known for its radicalism and heated debates on the future of revolutionary movements. Several alumni from this period—including Irving Kristol, Irving Howe, Daniel Bell, and Nathan Glazer—continued these discussions in the pages of the *Partisan Review* and other journals.

In addition to those already listed, well-known alumni of City College include several Nobel laureates as well as Upton Sinclair, A. Philip Randolph, Ira Gershwin, Edward Koch, General Colin Powell, and others.

Top: Shepard Hall, home to the School of Architecture, is one of the landmark neo-Gothic buildings of the North Campus Quadrangle which were designed by the noted architect George Browne Post. They are superb examples of English Perpendicular Gothic style.

Bottom: Statue of Alexander S. Webb, president of the College 1869–1902, who commanded the Philadelphia Brigade at Gettysburg.

The Cloisters

The Cloisters, a branch of the Metropolitan Museum of Art, is one of the few museums in the U.S. dedicated solely to medieval art.

Its combination of courtyards and medieval monastic gardens offers a fitting venue for the exhibits. Moreover, the location, with outdoor terraces and woods nearby, provides magnificent views of the Hudson River. No doubt the panoramic scene is a credit to John D. Rockefeller Jr.'s vision and the hard work of Frederick Law Olmsted Jr., son of the co-designer of Central and Prospect Parks, who reworked the rocky topography to preserve some of its pristine vistas.

The land where the Cloisters resides, Fort Tryon Park, was originally inhabited by the Weckquaesgeek Indian tribe native to the area. The park is named after Sir William Tryon, the last British governor of colonial New York.

Remaining rural for years, its views soon drew wealthy New Yorkers to its summit. In 1917, Rockefeller bought the property, as well as land on the New Jersey side of the Hudson to create Palisades State Park, preserving the area's views of the river below.

The Cloisters, situated at the northern end of Fort Tryon Park, opened to the public in 1938. The museum includes several cloisters, or courtyards, imported and assembled from French monasteries. It is perhaps most renowned for its collection of unicorn tapestries that were fabricated in Brussels circa 1500. Art historians estimate that it took over twenty years to complete the series.

Three of the reconstructed cloisters feature gardens planted according to horticultural information found in medieval treatises.

The Brooklyn Museum

The Brooklyn Museum was originally called the Brooklyn Apprentice's Library. Inspired, in part, by Benjamin Franklin's Apprentice's Library in Philadelphia, the founders here hoped to honor its spirit and create an institution to develop the moral education of local apprentices in the Brooklyn area.

The museum went through several name changes, including the Brooklyn Institute and the Brooklyn Institute of Arts and Science. Original plans called for a library-type institution. However, it was decided to model the Brooklyn Museum more closely after the Metropolitan Museum of Art and Museum of Natural History.

The museum occupies a building on Eastern Parkway that was built by the well-known architectural firm of McKim, Mead, and White in 1893. Its Beaux-Arts edifice builds on the design aesthetic of Frenchman J.N.L. Durand.

Over the years this edifice has changed to reflect the tenor of the times. Directors William Henry Fox and Philip Youtz, for instance, removed the grand staircase that graced its entrance in the 1930s to render the building more approachable by the public. Interestingly, late twentieth-century renovations by Arata Isozaki and James S. Polshek returned the building to some of its original details while holding onto the spirit of easy public accessibility. With its open windows and the playful grace of its water spouts, the entrance attracts crowds to its front entrance, tapping into the local spirit of community that the museum's mission has long supported.

The Brooklyn Museum does not shy from controversy nor cling to tradition. Its permanent collection ranges from twentieth-century American decorative art to ancient Middle Eastern pieces; it remains the second-largest art museum in New York.

Celebrated as an example of purely classical architecture, Low Memorial Library was completed in 1897 and served as the main library until 1934. Today this landmark building functions as the administrative center of the university. One of the most impressive features of Low is its rotunda topped by the largest all-granite dome in the country.

Columbia University

The oldest educational institution in New York State, Columbia University can trace its origins back to 1754 as Kings College under the royal charter of King George II.

Columbia's first president was Samuel Johnson, and the school opened its classes near Trinity Church in 1754 with an enrollment of fewer than ten students. Kings College was chartered as Columbia College in 1784 as part of a patriotic fervor that swept the young nation.

During the late nineteenth century, Columbia College distinguished itself by serving as one of the nation's earliest centers for graduate scientific education. It changed its name to Columbia University in 1896 and moved uptown to its present site in Morningside Heights. The first few decades of the twentieth century were noteworthy for the presence of notable thinkers and scholars like John Dewey, Franz Boas and Charles Beard. During the 1940s, the university hired a number of prominent postwar literary and cultural thinkers such as Lionel Trilling, C. Wright Mills, Jacques Barzun, and Richard Hofstadter.

Columbia and its campus have grown over the years. A few landmark buildings remain mostly intact. The Low Memorial Library is perhaps the most memorable visual symbol on campus, named not for its height but for its donor, former Brooklyn Mayor Seth Low. It served as Columbia's main library until 1934.

The campus, designed by McKim, Mead, and White, was planned as an urban academic village within a city, a spirit it retains to this day. However, the architects' original concept of a densely built campus, with a narrow central quadrangle and six intimate and sheltered side courts, was never followed. Only the court between Avery and Fayerweather Halls was completed, and this plan has been changed by the underground expansion of Avery Library.

The Frick Collection

The Frick Collection is housed in the former mansion of Henry Clay Frick. Frick's close business associations with Andrew Carnegie and J.P. Morgan brought this Pittsburgh, Pennsylvania, native to the City of New York. His Upper East Side home was built in 1913–14 by the firm Carrère and Hastings, who also designed the New York Public Library. The house sits slightly back from 5th Avenue and nearly stretches a full city block.

Frick died in 1919. On his death he bequeathed his mansion, collection, and $15 million to the City of New York. The Frick opened to the public in 1935. The intimate personal setting renders the Frick a unique museum. The building itself piques the historical imagination. An enclosed garden, which was added later, opens up the residential space to a beautiful skylight.

The collection emphasizes works from the Renaissance period. Giovanni Bellini, Titian, Jan van Eyck, Rembrandt, Jean Fragonard, El Greco, Pierre-Auguste Renoir, J.M.W. Turner, James McNeill Whistler, and Jan Vermeer are just some of the artists featured here.

In addition to the art, there is an impressive research library. The Frick Art Reference Library was founded in 1920 to serve scholars, art professionals, collectors, and students. The library's book and photograph research collections focus on European and American paintings, drawings, sculpture, prints, and illuminated manuscripts from the fourth to the mid-twentieth centuries.

It is said that Andrew Mellon was inspired by Frick's generous gift to the world, leading to his own contributions to the National Gallery of Art in Washington, D.C.

The West Gallery was planned from the start as an imposing setting, recalling the gallery of Hertford House (home of the Wallace Collection), those of English country houses, and ultimately the royal salons of the Renaissance and Baroque periods.

Lincoln Center for the Performing Arts

In 1959, President Dwight D. Eisenhower broke ground for Lincoln Center for the Performing Arts. According to the *Gotham Gazette*, the ceremony was marked by a grand performance, with a young Leonard Bernstein conducting Copland's *Fanfare for the Common Man* and a choir from Julliard singing Handel's "Hallelujah Chorus." The display matched the project's ambitions. The Lincoln Center complex became one of the largest performing arts centers in the world.

Lincoln Center was built on a site handpicked by public official Robert Moses. After completion, it assembled a group of companies in residence: the New York Philharmonic, the Metropolitan Opera, the New York City Ballet, as well as a theater organization, a library for the performing arts, a university, and a music school, all centered around a public plaza. True to its motivating principle, the center brought builders and business to revitalize the area.

Construction began in 1959 and took a decade to finish. The Philharmonic Hall (now known as Avery Fisher Hall) opened in 1962 with a wave of others to follow, including the Metropolitan Opera House, the New York State Theater, and the Julliard School, to name only a few. Lincoln Center's cultural hub would extend its reach farther, with its "Mostly Mozart Festival," "Live at Lincoln Center," and "Jazz at Lincoln Center" programs.

An array of architects were involved with the center including Max Abramowitz, Pietro Belluschi, Philip Johnson, and Wallace K. Harrison, among others. Many of the buildings offer a modern twist on a classical style. The spatial design includes a large square and marble fountain along with two other open spaces, Damrosch Park to the left of the Met, and the plaza in front of the Vivian Beaumont Theater, where in the center of the reflecting pool one will find *Reclining Figure*, a modern sculpture by Henry Moore.

Despite its monumental aspect, the complex, with its open spaces inviting exploration and forming the backdrop for open-air performances, remains true to its original aim of drawing the public into the arts.

The Metropolitan Opera House

Built in 1854, The Academy of Music at Irving Place and 14th Street was a sumptuous opera house for its time. There were about four thousand seats for the audience to enjoy opera, and only a handful of boxes for wealthy patrons. Increasing public demand for tickets led to a scarcity of seats that eventually motivated a group of New York industrialists and socially prominent families to establish the Metropolitan Opera House, a competing house to the Academy of Music.

The original design for the new opera house was created by J. Cleaveland Cady. Under the opening direction of Henry E. Abbey, the house featured Italian and French opera. The house soon turned to a German company to weather the early economic strain. In these years, it enjoyed seven seasons of German opera. After several years, French and Italian opera dominated the stage once again. Henry E. Abbey managed the company until his death in 1896.

Later manager Giulio Gatti-Casazza also played a notable role in the history of the Metropolitan Opera House. Under Gatti-Casazza, Arturo Toscanini and Artur Badansky served as conductors. He also introduced many artists to its stage, including Frances Alda, Lily Pons, Ezio Pinza, Giovanni Martinelli, Freidrich Schorr, Grace Moore, and many others.

At the start of the twentieth century, the opera house had become very popular with New Yorkers, especially new immigrants. Part of this spike in popularity was due to the fact that the Metropolitan Opera House broadcast a number of performances on the radio and, later in the century, on television.

Rudolph Bing served as manager in the 1950s and invited prominent conductors. Bing also supported the first black soloist, Marian Anderson, to perform, followed soon afterward by Leontyne Price.

The Metropolitan Opera House moved to Lincoln Center in 1966, and the old building in the Garment District was demolished. The building at Lincoln Center was designed by architect Wallace K. Harrison (who was part of the team that designed the United Nations Headquarters) and the lobby is decorated with murals by surrealist artist Marc Chagall. The Metropolitan Opera House remains the premier site in New York to enjoy opera.

The Metropolitan Opera House before a performance.

The Great Hall.

The Metropolitan Museum of Art

The Metropolitan Museum of Art is one of the leading museums in the world. Its permanent collection contains works from around the world, dating from ancient to contemporary times.

The project began in the mind's eye of John Jay in 1865 as a premier educational institution and cultural center; its board of trustees consisted of prominent businessmen and intellectuals including Jay, William Cullen Bryant, and Richard Morris Hunt.

According to its own literature, its first collection object, a Roman sarcophagus, was acquired in 1870, before it had a formal building to show it in. The museum moved to its Central Park location in 1880, a site chosen for its proximity to the park.

Calvert Vaux and Jacob Wrey Mould designed the Metropolitan Museum of Art's first permanent home—a red-brick neo-Gothic structure.

Little of it remains, but part of the original façade can be seen from the Robert Lehman Wing. Richard Morris Hunt designed the current central pavilion and the neoclassical façade. McKim, Mead, and White built two wings that would later house medieval and Renaissance works.

George Fiske Comfort, founder of the College of Fine Arts at Syracuse University, shepherded its early collections. The museum expanded rapidly with help from several benefactors. One of the earliest was J.P. Morgan, who donated European art and Egyptian artifacts.

As more works were added, more wings were built. In 1924, for example, an American wing opened that included paintings, sculpture, furniture, silverware, ceramics, and textiles—one of the largest of it kind in the world. The Metropolitan Museum of Art is also known for

The Roof Garden.

its extensive European painting collection and its collection of European armor from the Middle Ages and the Renaissance period. It houses dramatic exhibits as well—like the Temple of Dendur, a complete Egyptian temple that was transported to the museum from the Nile Delta and installed in the Sackler Wing in 1978.

The collection expanded considerably in 1969 when the museum acquired an assortment of works donated by Nelson A. Rockefeller, former U.S. vice president. They are housed in a wing named for Rockefeller's son, Michael C. Rockefeller. With works of art from all over the world including Africa, the Pacific islands, and pre-Columbian America and Asia, the breadth of its collections is amazing.

The museum regularly rotates its exhibits. As a result, only a small percentage of the museum's permanent collection is on view at any given time, but it is still impossible to view the Metropolitan Museum of Art's entire collection in a single day. It remains the largest and most comprehensive museum in the U.S. and one of the foremost in the world, with over two million works of art. It also operates the Cloisters in Fort Tryon Park.

Left: Detail of West 54 Street façade.

Opposite: View of the David and Peggy Rockefeller Building from The Abby Aldrich Rockefeller Sculpture Garden.

The Museum of Modern Art

The Museum of Modern Art (MoMA) is located at 11 West 53rd Street. It was founded in 1929 by Abby Aldrich Rockefeller (wife of John D. Rockefeller Jr.), Mary Quinn Sullivan, and Lillie P. Bliss. Its first major exhibition, featuring the work of Cezanne, Gauguin, Seurat, and van Gogh, was a harbinger of its important role in the art world.

According to historians, under its first director, Alfred Hamilton Barr Jr., the MoMA aimed to exhibit the full range of visual arts. It was a breadth of media which was unusual for the time. Its second director, Rene d'Harnoncourt, extended the collection to include abstract expressionism.

Now the MoMA has over 150,000 paintings, sculptures, drawing, prints, and photographs. It includes works by Jasper Johns, Frida Kahlo, Chuck Close, Paul Strand, Man Ray, and many others. Some of the most famous paintings in the field are here as well. Vincent van Gogh's *Starry Night*, for instance, and Pablo Picasso's *Demoiselles d'Avignon*.

Philip L. Goodwin designed the Museum of Modern Art building in 1939 on ground donated by the Rockefeller family. Philip Johnson added a new wing, years later, with two sculpture gardens designed by him as well.

In the late twentieth century, the museum was renovated. The new structure nearly doubled the size of the original. It combines innovative spaces with the MoMA's original architecture and sensibility. Through a series of full-length windows, Japanese architect Yoshio Taniguchi's emphasis on natural light opens the exhibit space up and offers powerful views of the Abby Aldrich Rockefeller Sculpture Garden.

From an opening collection of eight prints and one drawing, the Museum of Modern Art has grown to become the home of one of the most intriguing and inclusive collections of modern art in the world. By its own mission statement, it seeks to create a "dialogue between the established and the experimental, the past and the present." True to this aim, the MoMA remains responsive to the dictates of the field without losing its accessibility to a wide array of viewers.

The New School

The New School was formed in 1919 to present an educational alternative to other academic institutions in the city.

A private college with an original bent, it long drew exciting thinkers to its campus. Early faculty included Charles Beard, Thorstein Veblen, and John Dewey. Lewis Munford, John Maynard Keynes, W.E.B. Dubois, and many others gave courses or lectures at the school.

In the 1930s, the New School moved to 12th Street. The building there was designed by Joseph Urban and displays the work of José Clemente Orozco and Thomas Hart Benton within its walls. The relocation to Greenwich Village was significant. The school's collaborative spirit responded to community interests, particularly in the field of contemporary arts, where it served as a notable home to the "modernist" style in the visual and performing arts, from Martha Graham to Frank Lloyd Wright.

With its explicit mission of intellectual and academic freedom, the New School openly courted refugees during this period, particularly exiled Jews who were forced to leave Europe because of increased religious persecution—launching the "University in Exile" with the support of the Rockefeller Foundation. This mission continued later with the École Libre des Hautes Études and world-renowned scholars such as Claude Levi-Strauss.

Over the years, the New School retained its place on the cutting edge of academia. Refugee Erwin Piscator founded the Dramatic Workshop under the auspices of the New School which featured Tennessee Williams, Marlon Brando, Shelley Winters, Harry Belafonte, Tony Curtis, and many others. The New School widened public awareness and appreciation of psychoanalysis and feminist theory. Among those who lectured here in the 1950s are Hannah Arendt, Margaret Mead, and Karen Horney.

During the 1940s and 1950s, the school took on many of the trappings of a traditional college. By the end of the twentieth century, the institution had grown tremendously while retaining its mission as an innovative educational establishment, deeply connected to New York City. Originally called the New School for Social Research, the name was changed in 2005 to simply the New School.

Detail of a socially themed fresco by José Clemente Orozco (1883–1949), who was a leading member of the Mexican muralist public art movement, along with Diego Rivera and David Alfaro Siqueros.

Reading Room at New York Public Library.

The New York Public Library

Before the New York Public Library opened, the city had no major public library for its citizens. City residents used Astor and Lenox libraries. These suffered from inconsistent funding and their catalogues were often poorly organized. As a result, neither served New Yorkers as a true public institution.

The New York Public Library's beginnings were spurred by a trust set up by Samuel J. Tilden, former Democratic governor of the state. The site for the new building was chosen in an area next to Bryant Park occupied by a man-made lake. This once-critical reservoir collected fresh water from upstate New York.

The New York Public Library, designed by John M. Carrère and Thomas Hastings, opened to the public in 1911. Gradually the library increased acquisitions, extended hours, and opened its admissions policy.

Historians argue that recently arrived immigrants were among its earliest and most prominent beneficiaries, earning the institution the title of "people's university." One of the best known features from this era is the two lions, created by sculptor Edward Clark Potter, that grace the front entrance to the library. (Then) Mayor Fiorello La Guardia called them "Patience" and "Fortitude," traits he thought New Yorkers would need in order to persevere through the hardest days of the Depression.

In the decades following, the New York Public Library expanded its range of free programs to include concerts, dramatic readings, and lectures. Its numerous branch libraries aggressively focused on their service to local communities and the needs of ethnic minorities.

Four special research libraries have been established since: the Humanities and Social Sciences Library, the New York Public Library for the Performing Arts, the Schomburg Center for Research in Black Culture, and the Science, Industry, and Business Library.

The New York Public Library houses nearly fifty million items, ranging from the rarified to the everyday. It remains one of the more active and accessible public libraries in the world.

New York University

New York University, formed in 1831 as the University of the City of New York, stands as one of the largest private universities in the U.S. Its creation was led, in large part, by politician and intellectual Albert Gallatin, and it was founded with the aim of opening up educational opportunities to a range of New Yorkers.

By the 1890s, New York University attracted most of its students from the city proper. It adopted New York University as its name in 1896. NYU, as it is popularly known, sold its uptown University Heights campus (designed by Stanford White) in 1973 and began to settle itself downtown. New York University's Main Building

(1837) at 100 Washington Square East, between Waverly and Washington places, is one of its oldest campus structures to survive.

The late twentieth century saw New York University consolidate its presence near Washington Square Park. One of the more famous of these new structures, the Elmer Holmes Bobst Library, was designed by Richard Foster and Philip Johnson (of Museum of Modern Art fame).

A long-striving and great university, New York University attracts students and faculty from all over the nation and globe. The university rightly calls Greenwich Village its home and their futures are inextricably linked.

Washington Mews.

Radio City Music Hall

Radio City Music Hall at Rockefeller Center is one of the largest indoor theaters in the U.S. It has long been an elegant and beautiful place, affordable to the general public.

Radio City Music Hall opened in December 1932. Donald Deskey's Art Deco mix of luxurious and industrial materials embodies Radio City Music Hall's legacy as a place of magnificence. Its sumptuous foyer struck a positive and uplifting chord during the heart of the Depression. The hall's stage is one of the largest in the world. Its high ceilings, grand drapes, and 30-foot chandeliers allowed visitors a feeling of material comfort during the hardest of times.

For years, Radio City's program alternated between movies and live shows, but the venue became best known for its live spectacles. Frank Sinatra, Itzhak Perlman, and many others have all appeared in the hall. The regular performances of the Rockettes, a group of 36 dancers long associated with the hall, have come to symbolize the enduring glamour of Radio City Music Hall.

Although it remained widely popular well into 1970s, it was threatened with demolition more than once. Radio City Music Hall was declared a landmark in 1979 and its interior restored at a cost of $70 million. The neon marquee has been restored to its original red, blue, and gold glory. The Stuart Davis mural, *Men Without Women*, has been returned to its original home after almost 25 years at the Museum of Modern Art. The worn stage curtain has been replaced by a totally new one, woven in a pattern that enhances its shimmering glow.

The Solomon R. Guggenheim Museum

Founded by Solomon R. Guggenheim, the precursor to the modern-day Guggenheim Museum opened as the Museum of Non-Objective Painting in 1939. A museum of modern art, it began as a small collection that included the works of Paul Klee, Wassily Kandinsky, and a handful of others. The bulk of the early collection was amassed by baroness Hilla Rebay von Ehrenwiesen. Under her stewardship, the museum became a critical venue for aspiring artists to develop their craft.

According to historians, Hilla Rebay von Ehrenwiesen commissioned a building design by Wisconsin-born architect Frank Lloyd Wright at the request of Guggenheim. Wright generally disfavored the urban core as sites for his work, but he chose the museum's location on 5th Avenue and 88th Street because it was across the street from Central Park. Both Guggenheim and Wright would die before its completion. In 1949, Solomon Guggenheim's nephew Harry F. Guggenheim took over the institution and hired James Johnson Sweeney to replace von Ehrenwiesen. The new building opened in 1959.

With its steel frame and hand-plastered concrete spiral design, the Guggenheim building was considered a sculpture in its own right, a strangely organic form in the heart of the city. In 1992, a tower was built to supplement the original structure, shifting its circular aesthetic somewhat.

In 1976 Peggy Guggenheim, Solomon Guggenheim's niece, donated her home and collection in Venice to the museum. According to its own literature, the transcontinental collection helped form the basis for the Guggenheim's international ambitions. The Guggenheim has expanded to Spain and Berlin and is still growing.

The Solomon R. Guggenheim Museum was designated as a landmark in 1990.

The Whitney Museum of American Art

The Whitney Museum of American Art is the invention of Gertrude Vanderbilt Whitney. The first museum devoted exclusively to American art of the twentieth century, it was originally created to support the work of artists overlooked by mainstream institutions.

The story of the Whitney begins in 1929 when a collection of over 500 pieces belonging to Gertrude Vanderbilt Whitney was rejected by the Metropolitan Museum of Art. In response, Vanderbilt Whitney decided to create her own museum. The Whitney opened to the public in 1931 in four townhouses on 8th Street between 5th Avenue and MacDougal Street. Although Gertrude Vanderbilt Whitney died in 1942, the Whitney continued to grow. Its reputation played no small part in its expansion. The Whitney's collection was also buttressed by the help of a number of wealthy benefactors and individual donors.

The museum is located at 945 Madison Avenue in a building designed by Marcel Breuer and Hamilton Smith in 1966. This distinctive corner structure houses one of the most renowned and comprehensive collections of American artwork from the twentieth and twenty-first centuries. A must-see cultural site, it includes prominent pieces by Jasper Johns, Georgia O'Keeffe, John Sloan, Frank Stella, Edward Hopper, and many others.

Strolling Through New York's Favorite Neighborhoods

Astor Place

Astor Place is one of the more historic intersections of Greenwich Village. It was named after John Jacob Astor, the fur trader and real estate baron.

Astor Place's story begins in 1804, when John Jacob Astor bought a large tract of land just north of Great Jones Street. He turned it into a park called Vauxhall Gardens, a for-profit park area that attracted many of the well-to-do to move to the area, building wonderful new homes along Great Jones Street.

When real estate prices were at their peak in 1826, Astor decided to close down most of Vauxhall Gardens, dividing the property into plots for further development. Running a boulevard-like road down the center of the area — three blocks with no cross street — he named this area Lafayette Place. He priced the lots so that they would appeal only to the rich, and that he would make a very nice profit.

The famous Colonnade Row, built by Seth Geer, epitomized the concept of an ensemble row which was popular in nineteenth-century New York City. He bought up nine of Astor's lots on Lafayette Place's west side, and created one of the finest ensemble rows in the city. Built with a white marble façade of 28 marble columns that supported a running cornice overhang two stories above, it connected nine houses. Its architecture was altered drastically around the turn of

Previous page: Tompkins Square, East Village.

the twentieth century. Half of Colonnade Row was destroyed after five of the houses to the south were torn down to become a warehouse for Wanamaker's, the department store.

Meanwhile, on the other side of Lafayette Place was the Astor Library building, the precursor to the New York Public Library. Astor was persuaded by Washington Irving to bequeath funds for a free library, the first of its kind in the city.

Construction of the new library began two years after Astor's death in 1848, and the library opened its doors on January 9, 1854. It was later moved to newer, larger facilities. Eventually, it closed in May 1895.

When the city formed its Landmarks Preservation Commission, the Astor Library building was the first to be saved from demolition. It was declared a landmark in 1965. The commission converted the library into the Public Theater, which officially opened on October 17, 1967.

The glass kiosk that leads to the Astor Place subway stop is a replica of the original one: The previous kiosk was removed by the Metropolitan Transit Authority in 1967 as part of a $2.5 million station renovation that preserved the wall mosaics and terra-cotta plaques. Among the modern landmarks of Astor Place is the *Alamo*, a huge black cube set into the ground that folks love to spin.

Colonnade Row.

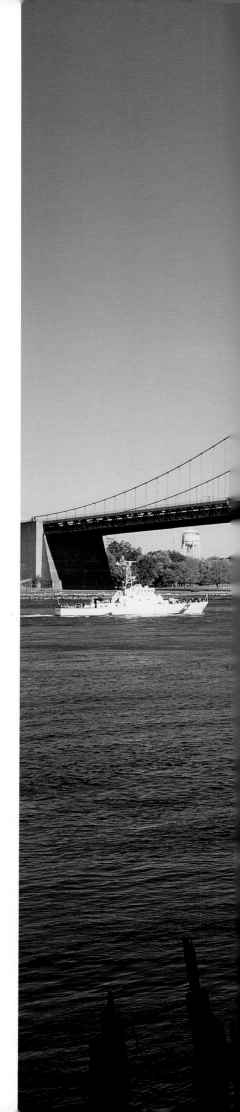

Left: Kaufman Astoria Studios in Queens.

Opposite: View of Triborough Bridge and Hell's Gate Bridge from Astor Park.

Astoria

Astoria is a neighborhood located in northwestern Queens, originally developed by Stephen A. Halsey, a fur merchant, in the late 1830s. According to some stories, residents wanted to name the area Sunswick, an Indian name, but Halsey persevered with his choice. He lobbied the state to name the area after fur trader and legendary New Yorker John Jacob Astor in the hopes that Astor would be moved by the gesture to provide the village's young ladies' seminary with funding. (Rumor has it that Astor relented with a sum of roughly five hundred dollars.)

The fate of the young ladies' seminary aside, Halsey's land purchase was a fortuitous one. A ferry station in Manhattan spurred growth in the area and it expanded dramatically during the 1840s. Its shore location proved critical to its development, and dangerous reefs were dynamited in the 1870s and 1880s to facilitate further growth.

Wealthy New Yorkers took to the bustling area and built mansions on and along 12th and 14th Streets. Meanwhile hardworking people sought their fortunes along its banks. German United Cabinet Workers were among them. They bought four farms in the area and developed a German town. Piano-maker William Steinway built factories along its shore as well. Steinway Village had its own foundries, factory, post office, parks, and housing for its employees.

While the famous piano factory of Steinway & Sons (1872) remains at the northwest corner of 19th Avenue and 38th Street, Astoria is also home to lesser-known industries like the Kaufman Astoria Studios, which housed Paramount Astoria Studios during the 1920s. These studios were home to films starring Paul Robeson and the Marx Brothers.

Overall, the appeal of Astoria can be found in its eclectic streets that mix residential and industrial buildings, with sophisticated designs abutting more ordinary ones. The architecture of Astoria is largely characterized by adjoining row houses and brick apartment buildings. A Greek influence dominates the neighborhood, from Greek-owned shops and community organizations to a series of impressive Greek Orthodox churches, including the renowned Saint Demetrious Cathedral, built in 1927.

Shopping on St. Marks Place.

East Village

The East Village used to be considered a part of the Lower East Side and the two share much common history. Home to successive waves of immigrants, the area had long been a dynamic working-class community. In the 1980s real estate developers began promoting the name East Village to dessociate the neighborhood from the Lower East Side's reputation as a slum district and to try to capture the cachet of Greenwich Village.

The area features a number of landmarks that illuminate parts of its early history. The Cooper Union for the Advancement of Science and Art, for instance, was established as one of the first colleges to offer a free education to the working-class. It also contains one of the oldest auditoriums in the United States. Before they were elected into office, Presidents Lincoln, Grant, Cleveland, Taft, and Theodore Roosevelt all spoke in the celebrated auditorium. The late twentieth century also saw two sitting presidents—Woodrow Wilson and William Jefferson Clinton—grace its Great Hall.

While Cooper Union speeches may have laid out American plans in the eyes of its elite, the nation's visionaries have also come from its streets. With Tompkins Square Park (1837) located in its immediate vicinity, the area quickly became a place of community for the working-class who lived there. Those who sought out Tompkins Square required relief from factory life and tenement living. Its public nature rendered it an ideal place to organize as well. Although Tompkins Square is known for its 1920s radicalism, militancy began much earlier. During the second half of the nineteenth century, for instance, protesters gathered in the park and marched on the New York Stock Exchange, and later, on City Hall.

During the late 1950s and 1960s, Tompkins Square became a mandatory stop on the countercultural trail. At the time, the East Village was legendary for its poetry and coffeehouses, book shops, theaters, and jazz clubs. Artists,

activists, and students found the grounds amenable to meeting. Groups participated in concerts, performance, and political actions in the park.

In the same tradition, during the 1980s, East Village residents mobilized around squatters' rights. The neighborhood's open opposition to the force of gentrification struck a unique chord. It came at a time when many other city squares and parks balked at the battles to preserve the diversity of their communities.

The Cooper Union for the Advancement of Science and Art.

Left: John Paul Jones Park, also known as Fort Hamilton Park and Cannonball Park, is the site of one of the world's last remaining Rodman guns, an 80-ton cannon produced during the American Civil War and the largest gun in the world at the time.

Right: Monument erected as a tribute to the American naval forces in Europe during World War II.

Bay Ridge

B ay Ridge is a neighborhood located in southwestern Brooklyn, named after a major glacial ridge that stretches the length of Long Island.

Originally dubbed "Yellow Hook" after the yellow clay of its shoreline, it was renamed Bay Ridge in 1853 because of the name's tragic suggestion of yellow fever. With its dramatic views and built-in respite from the city, Bay Ridge was a popular haven for prosperous New Yorkers after the Civil War.

Only a few of those mansions and summer homes remain as interesting architectural artifacts of the past: the Fontbonne Hall Academy and the intriguing Gingerbread House. The latter was built by J. Sarsfield Kennedy in the Arts and Crafts style in 1916–1917 and its Black Forest Art Nouveau architecture and simulated thatch roof earn it a spot on any historic guidebook list.

Perhaps the most secure remnant of the past is Fort Hamilton, named for Alexander Hamilton. Fort Hamilton remains the only active army post in the metropolitan area. Completed in 1831, it used to protect the harbor from Confederate ships during the Civil War.

Norwegian and Dutch immigrants settled in Bay Ridge during the early twentieth century followed soon by Italians, Greeks and those of Arabic descent. In the 1970s, the image of Bay Ridge changed when it became best known as the neighborhood where the film *Saturday Night Fever* was shot, superseding its old reputation as a summer resort. Eyes searching across the Upper New York Bay might be drawn less to its yellow clay than its spectacular view of the Verrazano-Narrows Bridge.

Right: The Bowery Savings Bank.

The Bowery and Downtown

The Bowery is a street that reaches from Chatham Square to Cooper Square, an abbreviated remnant of an old path used by indigenous people that stretched from Manhattan's southern to its northern tip. The name Bowery derives from *bowerij*, a Dutch word for "farm".

During Dutch rule, the area was dominated by farmland and then bought by Governor Peter Stuyvesant. As a principle north/south route, the area soon began to reflect the city's expansion. Theaters, oyster houses, and taverns cropped up alongside the road. A remnant from this period of commercial bustle, the Bowery Savings Bank, remains to this day. Designed by Stanford White, its uncompromising masonry exterior and detailed high arch suggest something of its once-solid dynamism as a commercial hub.

Famous for the Bowery Boys, nickel museums, and saloons, the area drew the destitute to its cheap flophouses for lodging. The area's struggle with poverty continued well into the twentieth century, particularly during the 1970s citywide fiscal crisis. Despite the hardships, the Bowery generated a creative culture such as the famed CBGB bar, which drew on its long tavern roots to become home to New York's vibrant punk rock scene. The Bowery's popularity in the twenty-first century as an upscale residential area is partly due to its proximity to Tribeca and SoHo.

Street scene on Greene Street, SoHo.

Right: London Terrace Gardens on 23rd Steet consists of 1,670 units. It was completed in 1930 and named for an 1845 strip of Greek Revival houses, also known as Millionaires' Row, designed by Alexander Jackson Davis. The doormen here used to dress like London bobbies.

Be sure to check out some of the excellent art galleries located around 23rd and 7th Avenue.

Chelsea

The name Chelsea was originally given by Captain Thomas Clarke to his 1750 estate, which covered the area from 19th to 28th streets, from 8th Avenue to the Hudson River. Clarke's grandson, Clement Clarke Moore, divided the estate into lots for development around 1830. Moore donated one block for use by the Episcopal Church's General Theological Seminary, which remains to this day on 9th Avenue between 20th and 21st streets.

From the middle of the nineteenth century until well into the twentieth century, Chelsea boasted a lively theater district. It was also home to a handful of small movie studios. Breweries, rail yards, and factories cropped up, particularly along Chelsea's Hudson River banks. In 1851, the Hudson River Railroad opened along 11th Avenue, and New York's first elevated rail-road opened in 1871. These lines are no longer in use, although portions of track remain along 11th Avenue.

Toward the nineteenth century's close, immigrants increasingly settled in the area and tenements were built to accommodate them. Some of these newcomers built churches that survive today. By the dawn of the twentieth century, Greeks represented the largest group of immigrants in the neighbor-hood, and several Greek-owned businesses opened on 7th Avenue.

As for Chelsea's border, the area once dominated by longshoremen had become the site of Chelsea Piers, which opened in 1910. Designed by the architectural firm of Warren and Wetmore, Chelsea Piers catered to passenger ship traffic and luxury liners, like the *Lusitania* and *Mauretania*. At one point, the piers fell into disrepair, but they were renovated in the 1990s as a sporting complex with a marina, bars, and restaurants.

Chelsea remains home to a diverse community of residents. Its hetero-geneity lives through landmark churches, historic brick homes, high-rise apartments, and art galleries that make it a signature neighborhood of the city.

Chinatown

Stretching across approximately two square miles bordering the Lower East Side, New York City's Chinatown is the largest Chinatown in the United States. According to historian Sarah Waxman, it is also the site of the highest concentration of Chinese in the Western Hemisphere.

Early Chinese settlers were primarily sailors and merchants. Most of these maritime workers were men who sojourned in the city only briefly. Some settled in the area; a smaller number stayed

and married. In the 1840s and 1850s, more and more Chinese started coming into this country from the West, seduced largely by the California Gold Rush and drafted by labor brokers to work the Central Pacific Railroad. Their original plan was to come to this country for a few years, earn enough money to take back to China, build a house, and marry. For this reason, the Chinese population in the United States was predominantly male.

The scarcity of gold in California, along with labor unrest, mob violence, and racial discrimination, caused an influx of Chinese migration eastward into Chinatown. Although many of those who lived in Chinatown worked in the maritime industry, by this time Chinese workers were gaining footholds in other industries as well, including hand-laundry, boarding house management, textiles, cigar-rolling, and restaurants.

Discrimination and increased anti-Chinese sentiment required that the Chinese band together to protect their own interests. Fraternal organizations, called "tongs," were formed to help Chinese settlers find jobs, get loans, mediate disputes, and protect themselves. The Chinese Consolidated Benevolent Association (CCBA) had its own constitution, levied taxes on all New York Chinese, and ruled Chinatown through much of the early half of the twentieth century, representing the Chinese elite; many other tongs formed protective and social associations for the working class.

In 1943, after Franklin Delano Roosevelt repealed the blatantly discriminatory Chinese Exclusion Act of 1882, Chinese immigration improved somewhat, albeit slowed down by strict quotas. Once quotas were abolished altogether in 1968, immigration dramatically increased. The borders of Chinatown spilled into Little Italy and the Lower East Side.

Many of the buildings in Chinatown are older tenements from the late nineteenth and early twentieth centuries. The area remains an architectural mix of old and new.

During the final decades of the twentieth century, the Chinese population expanded out from the island of Manhattan into its boroughs. Flushing, Sunset Park, and Bay Ridge are just a few neighborhoods that mark this demographic shift. At the same time, new immigrant communities — Vietnamese, Philippino, and Dominican, among others — have moved next to Chinatown. Despite these changes, Chinatown still represents one of the largest Chinese communities in the U.S.

Brooklyn Heights

Brooklyn Heights is a beautiful and historic neighborhood. The Heights extend from the Brooklyn Bridge south to Atlantic Avenue. On the east, its boundary is Cadman Plaza as far as Brooklyn's Borough Hall and then Court Street to Atlantic. The Esplanade, the walkway facing Manhattan, marks the western boundary. Brooklyn Heights commands a spectacular view of lower Manhattan. History abounds at every turn. It was here that George Washington slipped his troops across the East River while the English

Brick house in Brooklyn Heights.

slept. Even more august than its neighbor, Park Slope, the residential streets of Brooklyn Heights are lined with brownstones and mansions showing off a variety of architectural styles. The streets are a pleasure to walk along, and many are landmarked by the city. Visitors can stroll and shop along Montague Street. They can enjoy the shade of the neighborhood's trees and the serenity of its churches.

History buffs will enjoy the Brooklyn Historical Society on Pierrepont Street, a nationally renowned urban history center dedicated to the exploration and preservation of documents, artwork and artifacts representative of

View of Manhattan from Brooklyn Heights.

Brooklyn's diverse cultures past and present. Self-guided walking tours around the neighborhood are a tourist favorite, especially in the north section of Brooklyn Heights. Worthwhile stops include the First Presbyterian Church at 124 Henry Street, built in 1846, and the German Evangelical Lutheran Zion Church of 1840, situated on the same street.

Atlantic Avenue boasts Middle Eastern culinary delights and favorite local taverns. Brooklyn's Borough Hall is located just off Court Street, so named because of the Federal, City, and State Courts nearby.

One of the major draws for locals and visitors alike is the Promenade that gently winds its way along the East River against the backdrop of the Manhattan skyline. Like Manhattan's South Street Seaport, the Promenade pulls visitors back to the waterways that are central to New York's life. Popular for a casual stroll or run, one of the more intriguing places to visit is the foot of the Brooklyn Bridge. There, beneath this expansive structure, the engineering genius and majesty of the architecture reveals itself. Indeed, with all of these things to see, one can almost forget that the Brooklyn-Queens Expressway hums along busily above, a main transit artery between these two bustling boroughs.

Flushing Meadows

Flushing Meadows, part of north central Queens, was originally a woodland area blessed with an abundance of fresh water. Interestingly, its early population was more English than Dutch. When English Quakers bought the land during the 1650s, Governor Peter Stuyvesant was less than welcoming. According to historians, the Quakers' response to his displeasure, "The Flushing Remonstrance," stands as one of the first proclamations of religious freedom in the history of the United States. To this day, a Friends Meeting House preserves the architecture of one of New York City's oldest religious buildings. Built in 1694–95, by some accounts, it is one of the oldest houses of worship in continuous use in the United States.

Quaker tolerance reverberated beyond their immediate community to shape the demographics of the area. For one, Quakers drew African-Americans to Flushing in the nineteenth century, including inventor Lewis Latimer, who worked closely with Thomas Edison.

As in many of the outer boroughs, rail services brought expansion to Flushing during the nineteenth century. Mansions adorned the landscape after the Civil War. After World War II, apartment houses became a more common feature of city life. During the late twentieth century, one might have easily seen the rise of Buddhist houses of worship and Hindu temples. During the 1980s, Flushing became an attractive place for new arrivals to the U.S., including Chinese, Korean, Indian, and Colombian immigrants.

The neighborhood is best known for Flushing Meadows–Corona Park, the site of two World's Fairs. Only a few structures from these historic events remain standing today. Some are lesser-known but crucial markers of the past. One of these is the Whispering Column. Originally part of the Temple of Artemis, the ancient pillar was given to Flushing Meadows Park by King Hussein of Jordan during the 1964 World's Fair. The most visible landmarks are the observation towers and Unisphere, both of which dominate the area's skyline. Built by U.S. Steel, the Unisphere represents an especially interesting relic of the Cold War era. Its three rings around the globe symbolize the orbits of the first two American astronauts and the first Russian cosmonaut.

In addition, Flushing Meadows–Corona Park houses Shea Stadium, home of the New York Mets. A short walk from Shea Stadium is the U.S. Tennis Association's facility where the U.S. Open is played every year, attracting an international crowd of spectators.

Rocket Thrower *was created by Donald Delue (1897–1988) for the 1964 World's Fair and serves as the center of the Flushing Meadows–Corona Park fountain allée.*

The Unisphere, standing 140 feet high, was presented to the 1964 World's Fair by United States Steel. Today, it is Queens's most recognizable symbol. As the centerpiece for Flushing Meadows–Corona Park, it is the park's most popular meeting place.

The YMCA at 180 West 135ᵗʰ Street served as a training ground for artists and intellectuals.

Harlem

Once called Nieuw Haarlem by the Dutch who settled there, Harlem is one of Manhattan's most famous neighborhoods. Africans provided slave labor in Harlem when it was a Dutch farming colony. The original settlers were soon joined by a handful of wealthy residents who wanted to escape the city crowds. Many of these new inhabitants built estates in the area. Some of the estates, including the Morris-Jumel Mansion, remain standing.

An explosion in transportation during the late nineteenth century changed the landscape of the city, including its northern reaches. Farms gave way to broader settlement patterns, with apartments, brownstones and row houses to follow which attracted middle-class residents, many of whom were Protestant. However, a growing majority of residents were successful immigrants, including Eastern European Jews, who sought to escape overcrowded conditions downtown. By 1917, Harlem had the second-largest Jewish population in the U.S. Harlem's black population increased at the beginning of the twentieth century. The influx of black New Yorkers to the neighborhood reflected a slow demographic shift uptown, from residence downtown to San Juan Hill (replaced by Lincoln Square and Lincoln Center) and then to Harlem.

In the 1920s and 1930s, blacks came from other parts of the city, the American South, and the Caribbean; pushed out by discriminatory Jim Crow laws or attracted by the hope of greater economic opportunities. This was the famed Harlem of the 1920s, the Mecca of black political culture. Some landmarks for this era remain. One of these, the YMCA at 180 West 135th Street, was not only a prominent recreational and cultural center, but also served as a salon for a number of artists and intellectuals.

Although the Depression hit Harlem hard, the residents were determined to improve their quality of life. This indomitable spirit continued over the years during many battles for freedom. The speeches of community leaders such as W.E.B. Du Bois, Marcus Garvey, Father Divine, A. Philip Randolph, and Malcolm X, among others, provided inspiration. The neighborhood remains a central fixture of African-American culture, vibrant with politics and character.

A row of classic brownstones on Lenox Avenue in Harlem.

Greenwich Village

Called Sapokanican by the Canarsie Indians, Greenwich Village was once fed by a stream later dubbed Minetta Brook.

The area now known as Greenwich Village remained sparsely populated for much of the eighteenth century. By the 1780s, expansion compelled the city to purchase acres in an area that is known as Washington Square Park. For many years, this was used primarily as a potter's field and public gallows. Eventually, this once-secluded plot became a prime sight of development. With its suburban feel, however,

Christopher Street in Greenwich Village, site of the Stonewall Inn confrontation in 1969.

Building near Washington Square where the Triangle Shirtwaist Factory was located, the scene of the disastrous 1911 fire that took the life of 146 young women and heralded labor reforms across the nation.

the commercial activity struck a tempered chord. Stylish areas near 5th Avenue rose to meet the needs of Greenwich Village's wealthy residents. The row along the northern border of Washington Square Park has housed some of New York City's foremost merchants, bankers, and civic leaders.

New York University grew quietly on the east side of Washington Square in the nineteenth century and helped soften the neighborhood for literary salons and libraries. Soon, turn-of-the-century Greenwich Village became a vibrant community, home to a mix of African Americans, working-class immigrants, patricians and bohemians. Although freethinkers shaped the village's place in popular lore, its creative fount was the result of its full range of residents.

The artists and writers who arrived undoubtedly shaped the area with their "little magazines," galleries, and experimental theaters. The village is well associated with radical politics, from the left of Emma Goldman's years to the Stonewall Rebellion.

By its own account, Greenwich Village's historic district protects more than two thousand structures and encompasses one-third of the Village. Many visitors are drawn to its more famous sites like Washington Square Park and Judson Memorial Church. Some of its more enchanting treasures are tucked away in its mix of crooked lanes, from MacDougal Alley to Minetta Lane, home to one of New York's first black neighborhoods. Indeed, Greenwich Village is a rich weave of distinct sites that speaks to its long and varied past.

Kehila Kedosha Janina Synagogue on Broome Street.

The Lower East Side

The Lower East Side was originally home to the Kleindeutschland ("Little Germany") and Five Points neighborhoods. By the 1840s, the area's population had increased by 60 percent. During the 1880s, Italians and Eastern Europeans arrived. Some of the earliest tenements in the city were built here. Extraordinarily crowded and with poorly ventilated, tenements rarely had running water or toilets.

The Lower East Side was also rich with politics and culture. The neighborhood was the nexus of Jewish immigrant life in the nineteenth century, as Yiddish theaters, kosher food shops, Hebrew schools, synagogues, and other community staples were built. Many of these places faded in the late twentieth century as Jews enjoyed upward economic mobility and moved elsewhere. However, historical synagogues remain in the area, such the Angel Orensanz Center at 72 Norfolk Street and Kehila Kedosha Janina, the synagogue at 280 Broome Street that has received landmark status and a grant for restoration.

After the Second World War, the Lower East Side became far more ethnically diverse. The postwar period saw young artists and bohemians arrive as well. The area's secondhand bookstores and cafes nurtured the Beat Movement and Black Arts Movement. In the 1990s, gentrification of its textile factories and tenements into fashionable loft apartments and restaurants sparked a new wave of residents, attracting budding artists, musicians, progressives, and hipsters to its streets.

Fort Greene

Fort Greene was named after Nathaniel Greene, one of George Washington's top aides, who oversaw the construction of Fort Putnam on the hillock that is now Fort Greene Park.

By the start of the nineteenth century, the area's farms had been converted into a shipyard, and more grew rapidly along the riverbank. The plentiful work attracted a number of free blacks involved in the industry. Several structures from the period remain, including Hanson Place Baptist Church, which some say was an important stop on the Underground Railroad. Indeed, over time Fort Greene became a vibrant home to black residents and a hub of black culture.

The area is also home to a number of notable Brooklyn structures. One of these, the Brooklyn Academy of Music (BAM), on Lafayette Avenue and Ashland Place, is the Carnegie Hall of the borough. Fort Greene is also home to the tallest structure in Brooklyn, the Williamsburgh Savings Bank, built by George B. Post in 1929.

The Peter Jay Sharp Building, Brooklyn Academy of Music.

Prospect Park, built in the 1860s by Calvert Vaux and Frederick Law Olmsted, who also designed Central Park.

Park Slope and Prospect Park

Park Slope, a residential neighborhood in northeast Brooklyn, was once a thick woodlands and later, Dutch farming area. The Vechte-Courtelyou House, known popularly as the Old Stone House, is a replica of a Dutch farmhouse that played a role in the Battle of Brooklyn, during the American Revolutionary War.

Later, railroad owner Edwin C. Litchfield developed the area. His mansion, in use by the city park service, still sits on one of the highest points in Brooklyn overlooking Park Slope and Prospect Park. Land was sold block by block to

developers in the late nineteenth and early twentieth centuries. The city bought 526 acres of land to design Prospect Park, eventually giving the neighborhood its name. For its part, Prospect Park remains a central feature of the neighborhood. Built in the 1860s by Calvert Vaux and Frederick Law Olmsted, its bucolic expanse rises and falls around a series of ravines, lakes, and rustic areas. An enchanting space with horse walks, playgrounds, and ball fields, its popularity continues to increase.

Park Slope grew exponentially in the second half of the nineteenth century. In the late 1900s,

Park Slope was known as the Gold Coast for the gorgeous Victorian mansions built along Prospect Park West. Distinguished for having the largest landmark district in Brooklyn, Park Slope enjoys a wide architectural variety. Mansions rise on the park's western perimeter, particularly near Grand Army Plaza. Park Slope is lined with row houses and limestone buildings that once housed factory workers. Architectural styles of row houses and brownstones run from Neoclassical Italianate to Romanesque Revival. Striking buildings of note include the Montauk Club, designed by architect Francis H. Kimball, and the Fourteenth Regiment Armory on 14th Street.

The armory was home to the "Red-legged Devils" (a local company that served with merit during the Civil War), and it survives as one of the more architecturally intact National Guard armories in New York City.

The neighborhood also houses the central branch of the Brooklyn Public Library at Grand Army Plaza. Building of the Central Library at Grand Army Plaza began in 1912, but was not completed until 1941.

A fashionable enclave for artists, progressives, and bohemians during the 1970s, Park Slope has become increasingly middle-class and has attracted all manner of families with young children to purchase residences.

New York brownstones, Park Slope.

Off the Beaten Path:
Outer Islands

View of Hart Island from City Island.

City Island

City Island is located north of Pelham Bay Park in the Bronx. Before it was called by its present name, the land was referred to as Minnewits by local Siwanoy Indians; and later Minneford Island by the British.

The island was purchased by Benjamin Palmer in 1761. According to historians, Palmer hoped to challenge Manhattan's preeminence and renamed it City Island to attract metropolitan business. Although his strategy did not

succeed, the island sustained its own dynamic economy from the sea. About 1.5 miles in length, many residents fished, clammed, and dug oysters along its waterways. City Island was also the site of a major saltworks for the surrounding area.

A number of its residents were sailors and Execution Lighthouse and Stepping Stones Lighthouse are remnants of this navigational past. These sailors played a central role in navi-

Previous page: View of Manhattan from Roosevelt Island.

gating ships around the rocky reefs down the East River to safety in New York Harbor.

During the twentieth century, City Island became a popular summer resort for those wishing to escape the city. Yacht building had supplanted fishing, but the island remained a maritime community. Several yachts from the island won the prestigious America's Cup. During the First and Second World Wars, local industry shifted from yacht building to the construction of submarine chasers and other war vessels, returning to yacht-building activities after the war.

Easily accessible by water, the island still maintains a marina, an integral part of its strong nautical traditions, and it remains a surprising seacoast retreat within minutes of the bustling city. Its seafood restaurants are a popular local attraction.

Trinity Church, one of the three churches on City Island.

Coney Island

Coney Island used to be an island, until land-fill made it into a peninsula that connected it formally to the borough of Brooklyn. The Sea Gate community takes up the western tip, with Manhattan Beach on the far eastern edge, and Brighton Beach and Coney Island itself in the middle. But to sum it up in one word, it is FUN that attracts the entire world to Coney Island.

Since the 1800s, Coney Island has touched the hearts and sparked the imaginations of visitors and guests. It only cost a nickel to get to Coney Island on the subway, and once there, you were greeted by Nathan's Famous, home of the five-cent hot dog. From the recently renovated Steeplechase Pier to the Boardwalk, from the Parachute Jump to the classic Cyclone roller coaster, Coney Island has been home to some of the most exciting rides in the world. Even today, the Coney Island Cyclone remains popular with Brooklynites. The Parachute Jump is a 262-foot (80-meter) tower that featured a 250-foot (76-meter) drop in a seat for two. It operated between 1939 and 1968 and became a New York City landmark in 1988.

The New York Aquarium began in Battery Park in 1896, where it stayed until 1941. After a temporary stint at the Bronx Zoo, it found its permanent new home on Coney Island in 1955; then and now, it continues to wow, entertain, and educate.

The hot dog was invented in Coney Island by a Polish immigrant and entrepreneur named Nathan Handwerker, whose 5-cent hot dogs became world famous. Every Fourth of July, Nathan's Famous hosts the International Hot Dog Eating Contest that attracts weiner-wolfers from all over the world.

Since the Depression, Coney Island has suffered an economic decline, but happily it is undergoing a major renaissance, spurred by

public and private interests who wish to bring Coney Island back to its original glory as a "Fiefdom of Fun."

This modern revival includes zany events like the Mermaid Parade, officially opening the summer swimming season. The Mermaid Parade combines a variety of different elements from maritime mythology and Mardi Gras to create a good time for all.

In 2001, The Brooklyn Cyclones minor-league baseball team brought baseball back to Brooklyn after a 44-year hiatus. They play to packed houses in KeySpan Park, giving New Yorkers that good old-fashioned baseball experience that is often lost in big league ball-parks.

Opposite: A view of the KeySpan Park field during a night game, July 2004. KeySpan Park, home to the Brooklyn Cyclones, is located in Brooklyn's famous Coney Island.

Above: Coney Island, amusement park.

Ellis Island

Originally a small sandbar that was barely detectable in the high tide, Ellis Island became the gateway to America. It has a history that spans hundreds of years. Originally called Kioshk, or "Gull Island," by the Mohegan Indians, it had several names given to it by its conquerors and settlers; according to some, it was even christened Gibbet Island, after the gibbet, an instrument used to hang people (a common activity on the island during the 1760s).

Owned by Samuel Ellis in the 1770s (from whom it received its final name) and then the

Ellis Island Immigration Museum.

Looking for relatives on the American Immigration Wall of Honor, which contains over 600,000 names of individuals and families who immigrated to the United States.

U.S. War Department, it became a fort to defend the harbor. In 1892, Ellis Island took on its best-known role. It replaced Castle Garden as New York's immigration center because Battery Park had become too small to handle the growing numbers of immigrants arriving on New York's shores. To accommodate the shift, work had to be done on the island itself. Ellis Island was enlarged by landfill, so that its original three acres grew to over 25 in the decades that followed. Landfill was made partially from the ballasts of old ships, but mostly from discarded fill from the construction of the New York subway system.

From 1892 to 1924, over 15 million immigrants entered the U.S. at Ellis Island. According to statistics, nearly 40 percent of all living Americans can trace their roots to an ancestor who came through Ellis Island.

Ellis Island was officially closed by the government during the 1950s. Nearly ten years later, President Lyndon Johnson declared Ellis Island part of Statue of Liberty National Monument, but it sat neglected for years. Work was done to refurbish Ellis Island during the 1980s. The renovated main building houses an excellent museum on immigration history.

Liberty Island / Statue of Liberty

Liberty Island, the home of the Statue of Liberty, lies in New York Harbor, a short distance from the tip of Manhattan.

Before it was renamed Liberty Island in 1956, the island sported a great many names, including Minnissais, Great Oyster, Love Island, Kennedy's Island, Corporation Island, and Bedloe's Island. Its uses were equally diverse. At one time or another, Liberty Island served as a quarantine spot, a pest house, a refuge for British loyalists,

and a hospital. After the United States gained independence from the British Empire, Bedloe's Island served as a defense fortification to protect New York Harbor.

The Statue of Liberty was borne out of diplomacy, not defense. The monument represented a joint building effort between the United States and France. Its structural iron framework was designed by Gustave Eiffel and the statue's form was designed by sculptor Frederic-Auguste Bartholdi. The pedestal, on the other hand, was an American venture. Joseph Pulitzer headed the effort to finish the pedestal in 1885. It was designed by Richard Morris Hunt, who also worked on the Metropolitan Museum of Art.

The "Lady in the Harbor," as she is known, stands 101 feet tall (30.78 meters) from base to torch, 305 feet tall (92.96 meters) from pedestal foundation to torch. She posseses a 35-foot (10.67-meter) waist and an 8-foot (2.4-meter) index finger, and weighs 450,000 pounds (204.11 metric tons).

The Statue of Liberty was officially dedicated in 1886. An important diplomatic monument, it held special significance for immigrants as well. One of the first images they saw of America from aboard ships, the monument long stood as a symbol of opportunity and hope. Repair work on the Statue of Liberty periodically has taken place over the last twenty years. After 9/11, the island was closed to tourists for security reasons, but it was reopened in 2004 .It remains a popular site for visitors and a powerful symbol of the nation's ideals.

Roosevelt Island

Dutch Governor Wouter Van Twiller bought Minnahannock Island in 1637 from two chiefs of the Canarsie tribe. *Minnahannock* means "It's Nice to Be Here" or "Long Island," the latter readily explained by the dimensions: 107 acres (later expanded to 147), 2 miles long, 800 feet wide at its broadest width. The Dutch raised hogs on the island, so it became known as Varcken ("Hog") Island. Subsequent owners included Captain John Manning and then Robert Blackwell, who farmed the land. Blackwell House is one of the few farmhouses in the city that dates back to the Revolutionary War.

In 1828, the City of New York acquired the island and used the space to house municipal institutions such as prisons, poorhouses, and nursing homes that were later relocated to other parts of the city. Some structures from the nineteenth century remain, like Blackwell Lighthouse at its northern tip, but Renwick Ruin might be the most dramatic among them. The castle-like structure (circa 1850) lies at the opposite end of Roosevelt Island. Renwick is named after the architect James Renwick Jr. (architect of St. Patrick's Cathedral). Originally the building served as a smallpox hospital.

It was not until the start of the 1970s that Roosevelt Island developed its modern incarnation as a quasi-suburban haven. Under the direction of Mayor John Lindsay and with the help of the Urban Development Corporation, the city slowly transformed the island into a popular residential community.

The change took time; a subway to the area opened as late as 1989. Before then, an aerial tramway was the only access from Manhattan. Today, automobiles are allowed on the island, but their use is limited. With its quieted pace and magnificent views, Roosevelt Island comfortably stands as a residential island enclave in the heart of one of New York's major waterways.

Staten Island

Staten Island is New York's most southern and suburban borough. Its history parallels the story of many neighboring islands that had an early emphasis on farming and fishing. A visitor can still get a taste of that past in places like Snug Harbor, located in the national landmark district of the island, and the beautiful and spacious Gateway National Recreation Area. Richmond Town is a popular outdoor museum where visitors glimpse life on the island from the past two centuries. Like Manhattan, the island features a military past as well, still very much alive in Fort Wadsworth.

The island was visited by Henry Hudson in 1609 and was called Staaten Eylandet by the Dutch. The indigenous population drove off the first white settlers, but by 1661 a permanent European settlement had been founded. Although there was considerable industrial activity on Staten Island in the nineteenth century, its predominant character was semirural, something which did not change when it became a borough of New York City in 1898.

The turning point in the island's recent history was the completion of the Verrazano-Narrows Bridge in 1964. Since then Staten Island has had an influx of new residents and industries. Changes in the 1980s to the structure of New York City's government led many Staten Islanders to believe their voting strength was being diminished. In 1993, Staten Island residents voted to secede from the city, but no official succession took place because the New York State government did not grant approval.

Built in 1892, the Music Hall at Snug Harbor Cultural Center is a fine example of Greek Revival architecture.

Fort Wadsworth battery.